MONTGOMERY COLLEGE LIBRARY
GERMANTOWN CAMPUS

CORNELL STUDIES IN CIVIL LIBERTY

ROBERT E. CUSHMAN, *Advisory Editor*

CIVIL LIBERTIES IN THE UNITED STATES

A Guide to Current Problems and Experience

CIVIL LIBERTIES IN THE UNITED STATES

A Guide to Current Problems and Experience

By ROBERT E. CUSHMAN

Goldwin Smith Professor of Government
Cornell University

CORNELL UNIVERSITY PRESS

Ithaca, New York

Reprinted with the permission of Cornell University Press

JOHNSON REPRINT CORPORATION / JOHNSON REPRINT COMPANY LIMITED
111 Fifth Avenue, New York, N.Y. 10003 / Berkeley Square House, London, W. 1

© 1956 BY CORNELL UNIVERSITY

CORNELL UNIVERSITY PRESS

First published 1956

17578

First reprinting, 1965, Johnson Reprint Corporation
Printed in the United States of America

Introduction

THE directors and officers of The Fund for the Republic asked me to prepare for their use, and perhaps for somewhat wider circulation, a summary which would present a bird's-eye view of the entire field of civil liberties since the close of World War II. This is designed to be an outline of the entire area with perhaps just a little meat on the bones. It seeks to include all of the problems which lie in this field, except those listed on page vii, and to place them in their proper context.

In dealing with each problem, I have sought to do three things: first, to indicate the status of each civil liberty at the close of World War II; second, to summarize the principal developments with respect to these liberties during the last decade; and third, to indicate in each case what the current or unsolved problems appear to be, together with some of the more important proposals for dealing with them which have been put forward. I have not undertaken to volunteer solutions of my own.

There is probably no complete common agreement upon just what the term "civil liberties" should include, although there is a well-recognized central core upon which there would be no dispute. At the fringe of the field, however, the term "civil liberties" may be a question-begging word, since some people, viewing a particular situation, would deny that any civil liberty problem was presented by it. I have not attempted to solve this problem by setting up any definitions; rather I have sought to include in this summary some mention of every subject which is regarded as a civil liberty problem by any articulate group or minority. The inclusion of a topic of this sort therefore does not imply any judgment of my own with respect to it.

A summary as comprehensive as this, yet a summary kept brief so that it can be used as an outline, may seem to have some of the earmarks of dogmatism. Very concise statements about important problems omit, of necessity, the qualifying comment necessary for complete accuracy. To present my opinion is not, however, the intent of this survey; my intent is to present the factual material, assembled with every effort to make it accurate. Limitations of space allow only meager documentation. Nevertheless, while I have sought to avoid slanting my comments upon the many controversial problems here dealt with, it could be that, as one who has spent many years working in the civil liberty field, I shall not have succeeded entirely in concealing a bias in favor of the adequate protection of civil liberty.

The order in which the problems are here presented is more or less arbitrary. It does not rest upon any philosophy of relationships between them. I have begun with the civil liberties protected in the First Amendment in our Bill of Rights—freedom of speech, press, religion, and assembly—described by Justice Cardozo as being "of the very essence of a scheme of ordered liberty." Further, the civil liberty

INTRODUCTION

problems generated by our current drive to protect our internal security against communism stand out sharply enough to warrant separate treatment, and I have therefore devoted a section to them. Many of these problems are, however, merely special examples or forms of well-known civil liberty problems such as those which relate to freedom of speech and the rights of persons accused of crime, and I have resorted to rather elaborate cross referencing in order to avoid duplication of treatment.

Certain things have been omitted from this summary, perhaps a bit arbitrarily. First, I have not dealt with political rights, such as the right to vote or hold office or be represented fairly in legislative bodies, since these are not commonly classified as civil liberties. In the second place, the problems dealt with are those which exist in the civil life of the country and not the special problems which arise in its armed forces. Since the war there have been significant improvements in the management of courts martial, and perhaps of other rights and privileges of men in the armed forces. These, too, are beyond the scope of this study. Third, I have not discussed individual economic rights, such as the "right to work," as affected either by law or by labor union rules. Finally, I have omitted consideration of the declaration of human rights in the United Nations and of similar matters which lie outside the domestic field.

Ithaca, New York   ROBERT E. CUSHMAN
April 10, 1956

Table of Contents

INTRODUCTION..............................	v
I. FREEDOM OF SPEECH, PRESS, ASSEMBLY, AND PETITION....................................	1
A. GOVERNMENTAL RESTRICTIONS....................	2
1. PROTECTION OF PUBLIC SECURITY.............	2
2. PROTECTION OF THE ADMINISTRATION OF JUSTICE	8
3. PROTECTION OF PUBLIC MORALS AND DECENCY...	11
4. PROTECTION OF PRIVATE INTERESTS AGAINST LIBEL AND SLANDER............................	19
5. PROTECTION AGAINST SPEECHES AND PUBLICATIONS ALLEGED TO BE NUISANCES.................	26
6. ASSURANCE OF THE POLITICAL NEUTRALITY AND LOYALTY OF PUBLIC EMPLOYEES.............	28
7. POSTAL CENSORSHIP AND ALLIED PROBLEMS......	30
8. FREE SPEECH AND PRESS IN LABOR RELATIONS....	48
B. FREE SPEECH AND PRESS IN THE COURTS...........	55
1. ATTITUDE OF THE SUPREME COURT, 1945–1950...	55
2. CHANGES IN THE SUPREME COURT'S ATTITUDE SINCE 1950.....................................	57
C. FREEDOM OF ASSEMBLY.........................	60
D. FREEDOM OF PETITION.........................	63
1. PETITIONS NOT CONTEMPTS OF COURT..........	64
2. LOBBYING.................................	65
3. GUILT BY ASSOCIATION......................	65

E. Private Curbs on Speech and Press	66
SELECTED READINGS	68

II. ACADEMIC FREEDOM 70
A. Distinctions between Educational Institutions — 71
1. denominational schools 71
2. tax-supported colleges and universities 71
3. tax-supported public schools 73
B. Basic Code of Academic Freedom 73
1. freedom of speech, writing, and research 73
2. freedom of public discussion in the academic community 74
3. textbooks, teaching materials, and curriculum 75
4. the teacher as a citizen—political activity and associations 75
5. tenure of teachers 76
6. freedom for students 77
C. Current Problems of Academic Freedom 80
1. loyalty oaths for teachers 80
2. dismissals on loyalty grounds 81
3. congressional investigations of schools and colleges 83
4. teachers who invoke the fifth amendment .. 84
5. controls on loyalty grounds of other interests 85
6. secrecy—classified research on the campus ... 86
7. dangers to academic freedom from those who finance education 87
8. impact on academic freedom of outside pressure groups 89

SELECTED READINGS 90

III. FREEDOM OF RELIGION: SEPARATION OF CHURCH AND STATE 92
A. Protection of Religious Opinion from Governmental Abridgment 92

CONTENTS

1. RELIGIOUS FREEDOM NOT A PROTECTION OF ANTI-SOCIAL CONDUCT.......................... 92
2. "PREFERRED STATUS" ACCORDED TO RELIGIOUS BELIEF AND ITS EXPRESSION................. 94
3. CONSCIENTIOUS OBJECTORS.................... 94
B. SEPARATION OF CHURCH AND STATE.............. 99
1. STATE AID TO PAROCHIAL SCHOOLS.............. 100
2. RELIGIOUS INSTRUCTION IN PUBLIC SCHOOLS...... 102
3. MERGERS OF SECTARIAN AND PUBLIC SCHOOLS..... 104
4. MISCELLANEOUS GOVERNMENTAL RECOGNITIONS OF RELIGION................................... 106
SELECTED READINGS.......................... 107

IV. THE RIGHT TO SECURITY AND FREEDOM OF THE PERSON................................. 109
A. THE RIGHT OF HABEAS CORPUS.................. 109
1. FEDERAL HABEAS CORPUS FOR PRISONERS HELD UNDER STATE AUTHORITY................... 109
2. SUSPENSION OF THE WRIT OF HABEAS CORPUS...... 111
B. FREEDOM OF MOVEMENT AND RESIDENCE........... 112
1. FREEDOM OF MOVEMENT WITHIN THE COUNTRY... 112
2. FREEDOM TO LEAVE THE COUNTRY—THE RIGHT TO A PASSPORT................................ 113
C. PROTECTION AGAINST SLAVERY AND PEONAGE...... 117
D. PROTECTION AGAINST LYNCHING.................. 120
1. LYNCHING AS A NATIONAL CIVIL LIBERTY PROBLEM 120
2. METHODS PROPOSED FOR FEDERAL CONTROL...... 121
3. CONSTITUTIONAL DOUBTS ABOUT FEDERAL CONTROL 122
E. THE CIVIL RIGHTS SECTION IN THE DEPARTMENT OF JUSTICE...................................... 124
1. BACKGROUND............................... 124
2. CIVIL RIGHTS SECTION....................... 125
F. EMERGENCY DETENTION UNDER THE INTERNAL SECURITY ACT OF 1950............................. 128
SELECTED READINGS.......................... 130

V. MILITARY POWER AND CIVIL LIBERTY...... 131
SELECTED READINGS.......................... 134

VI. THE CIVIL LIBERTIES OF PERSONS ACCUSED OF CRIME 135
A. Securing the Evidence 135
1. UNREASONABLE SEARCHES AND SEIZURES 135
2. WIRETAPPING 138
3. SELF-INCRIMINATION 140
B. The Arrest 146
C. The Accusation 147
1. INDICTMENT BY GRAND JURY 147
2. THE RULE AGAINST VAGUENESS 148
D. The Trial 149
1. TRIAL BY JURY 149
2. THE RIGHT TO COUNSEL 153
3. CONFRONTATION OF WITNESSES 155
4. ESSENTIAL FAIRNESS REQUIRED BY DUE PROCESS OF LAW 156
E. Cruel and Unusual Punishments 157
F. Double Jeopardy 158
G. Ex Post Facto Laws and Bills of Attainder 160
1. EX POST FACTO LAWS 160
2. BILLS OF ATTAINDER 162
H. Treason 163
SELECTED READINGS 164

VII. CIVIL LIBERTIES AND NATIONAL SECURITY 166
A. Scope and Nature of Our Program to Protect Our National Security 167
1. COUNTERESPIONAGE 167
2. LAWS TO PROTECT THE NATION'S SECRETS 167
3. LAWS TO PREVENT ALIEN SUBVERSION 168
4. LOYALTY AND SECURITY PROGRAMS 169
5. LOYALTY OATHS 172
6. CRIMES AGAINST NATIONAL SECURITY, FEDERAL AND STATE 175
7. DISCLOSURE REQUIREMENTS FOR SUBVERSIVES OR POTENTIAL SUBVERSIVES 175
8. DISABILITIES IMPOSED ON SUBVERSIVES 176

CONTENTS

  9. LEGISLATIVE COMMITTEES INVESTIGATING SUBVERSION.................................... 177
  10. PRIVATE ACTIVITIES DIRECTED AGAINST COMMUNISM AND SUBVERSION......................... 177
 B. Deviations from Traditional Civil Liberty Principles.................................. 177
  1. THE DOCTRINE OF SEPARATION OF POWERS....... 180
  2. DEFINITENESS OF LOYALTY AND SECURITY STANDARDS 181
  3. PRESUMPTIONS OF GUILT—"GUILT BY ASSOCIATION" 185
  4. LACK OF PROCEDURAL FAIR PLAY.............. 191
  5. "JUSTICE BY POLITICIANS" IN OUR PROGRAM AGAINST SUBVERSION............................... 198
  6. PRIVATE EFFORTS TO COMBAT COMMUNISM AND SUBVERSION............................... 201
 SELECTED READINGS......................... 205

VIII. CIVIL LIBERTIES OF ALIENS................. 208
 SELECTED READINGS......................... 210

IX. RACIAL DISCRIMINATION..................... 211
 A. Discrimination against Negroes............... 211
  1. STATUS AT THE END OF WORLD WAR II........... 211
  2. DEVELOPMENTS SINCE 1945.................... 213
  3. THE SCHOOL SEGREGATION CASES OF 1954........ 221
  4. IMPLEMENTING THE SCHOOL SEGREGATION CASES.. 224
 B. Discrimination against Jews.................. 225
 C. Discrimination against Other Racial Minorities 228
 SELECTED READINGS......................... 229

TABLE OF CASES............................. 231

INDEX...................................... 237

CIVIL LIBERTIES IN THE UNITED STATES

A Guide to Current Problems and Experience

· I ·

Freedom of Speech, Press, Assembly, and Petition

Congress shall make no law ... abridging the freedom of speech, or of the press; or the right of the people peaceably to assemble, and to petition the Government for a redress of grievances.—U.S. CONSTITUTION, FIRST AMENDMENT

PROVISIONS similar to this are found in the constitutions of most of the states. Since 1925 the guarantees in the First Amendment apply to the states through the due process clause of the Fourteenth Amendment, which provides: "...nor shall any State deprive any person of life, liberty, or property, without due process of law...." Thus the states are under federal judicial discipline in the matter of these rights. (*Gitlow* v. *New York,* 268 U.S. 652, 1925.)

These guarantees are protections against governmental violations of the rights of free speech and press; the governments of both state and nation are forbidden to violate these rights. Protection against their invasion by private persons, however, is placed, not in constitutions, but in such criminal and civil statutes as the national and state governments may validly pass.

First Amendment rights are, of course, not absolute and were never intended to be so. They are relative, in the sense that they are limited by the coexisting rights of others (as in the matter of libel) and by the demands of national security and public decency. Civil liberty issues are heavily involved when one is drawing the line which separates the speech and publication which government must suppress in order to be safe and decent from that which it must allow and protect in order to be free and democratic. First Amendment rights are abridged if governmental restraints on freedom of expression are more severe than legitimate community interests justify, or if these restraints are applied arbitrarily in individual cases.

A. GOVERNMENTAL RESTRICTIONS

1. Protection of Public Security in Peace and War

a. *Carry-over of Wartime Restraints on Speech and Press*

It has never been questioned that war, with its threats to the safety of the nation, justifies limits on freedom of speech and press. But war in the legal sense does not always end when the fighting stops. The Espionage Act of 1917 (which forbids speech and publication obstructing the war effort, interfering with recruiting, and encouraging evasion of the draft) was by the nature of its provisions intended to be applicable only in time of war. It remained dormant between the two world wars. But after World War II, Congress ordered it continued in force until six months after the end of the emergency proclaimed by the President in 1950, unless Congress should end the emergency sooner. There is, however, no record of prosecutions under the Act since the end of open hostilities in 1945.

Treason (discussed more fully *infra,* p. 163) is by definition a war crime. It consists of levying war against the government or giving aid and comfort to its enemies. The wrong kind of speech, that which gives "aid and comfort," is treason; and eight of the government's prosecutions for treason in World War II were for broadcasting for either Germany or Japan. Constitutional amendments offered in 1955 would make treason a peacetime crime. These would add to the treason clause the crime of "adhering to any group which advocates the overthrow of government by force and violence." The obvious purpose is to declare Communists to be guilty of treason.

b. *Sedition—Crimes of "Advocacy"*

Walter Gellhorn has defined sedition as follows:

The crime of sedition consists of advocacy by word of mouth, publication, or otherwise which incites discontent and contempt for the present form of government, causing persons to flout its laws and tending to destroy the government itself. It includes advocacy which incites to overthrowing the existing government, by force and violence, to bring into contempt the form of government, its public officers, its military forces, flags, and other symbols.

No overt act is required for the commission of sedition. Mere advocacy alone which is likely to incite is the essence of the crime. [Gellhorn, *States and Subversion,* p. 397.]

The Smith Act, passed in 1940, is the first federal peacetime sedition act since the ill-fated Sedition Act of 1798. The Smith Act confines itself essentially to forbidding the advocacy of the overthrow of government by force or violence and conspiracies to bring this about.

Forty-five states in the Union have laws designed to

serve the same end. These vary widely. Their texts range all the way from the fairly clear language of the Smith Act (copied largely from a New York statute of 1902) to the fuzzy provisions of the West Virginia statute which make it "unlawful to speak, print, publish or communicate ... any teachings, doctrines or counsel in sympathy with or in favor of ideals, institutions or forms of government hostile, inimical or antagonistic to those now or hereafter existing under the Constitution and laws of this state or of the United States." (W. Va. Code, 1937, §5912.)

Ardent defenders of civil liberty persist in doubting the necessity and therefore the justification for sedition laws; while not denying the right of government to protect itself, they argue that present criminal statutes forbidding incitement to crime already provide full protection against really dangerous speech and that if speech is not dangerous in the sense of being incitement it should not be forbidden. Public opinion, however, has left those who share this view far behind and has come to accept the propriety of legislation of this type, especially as public concern about communism and possible espionage has mounted.

No carefully drawn sedition statute has thus far been held unconstitutional *per se*. Badly drawn sedition statutes have been invalidated on grounds of vagueness and uncertainty. *(Herndon v. Lowry,* 301 U.S. 242, 1937; *Stromberg v. California,* 283 U.S. 359, 1931.) It is possible that such a fate might await the West Virginia provision just quoted.

The civil liberty problems posed by these sedition and "advocacy" laws fall in the area of their enforcement. To apply a valid statute to a case not properly within its scope is to deny First Amendment rights. See the later discussion (p. 55) of the judicial interpretation of all of these laws.

c. *Registration and Disclosure Requirements*

It is an obvious restraint upon complete freedom of speech and press to be required by law to identify or label oneself in a manner deemed derogatory. In dealing with limited groups, however, Congress has set up such requirements, as follows:

The Foreign Agents Registration Act of 1938, later amended, requires that the agent of any foreign power or group must register with the Attorney General and that political propaganda sent by such agents through the mails or through interstate commerce must be labeled to show that it is sent by a person so registered. It is a crime to evade these requirements, and the Postmaster General may bar from the mails any matter sent from abroad by persons not so registered. This all seems proper enough. Civil liberty problems may, however, arise here. In 1951 five persons—officers of the Peace Information Center—were indicted under this statute for not having registered as foreign agents. The government's position was that the propaganda of this organization paralleled that of the Russian peace drive and justified the inference that these persons were therefore agents of the Soviet Union. They were acquitted on the ground that the fact of this agency was not shown. The government's interpretation of the Act appears to be that any material emanating from a foreign principal, even without the intervention of an agent in this country, is assumed to come through a hypothetical agent.

The Subversive Activities Control Act of 1950 requires that all literature distributed by, and all radio and television broadcasts made by, registered Communist organizations must indicate that they are disseminated by or sponsored by such Communist organizations. The law sets up elaborate administrative and judicial procedures for identifying these organizations as Communist and compelling them to register. The constitutionality of this statute was argued in the Supreme Court late in 1955 (p. 176).

d. *Government Secrecy Rules—Censorship at the Source*

Freedom of the press is in theory impaired by restrictions upon the right or opportunity of newspapers to acquire and publish information of public interest. In practice, there have always been secrets which the government, in the public interest, has felt it necessary to keep.

No one quarrels with security rules reasonably designed to protect the national safety and to prevent information from falling into the hands of foreign countries to be used to our disadvantage. A thick blanket of secrecy, thought by some to be much too thick, has been wrapped around most of our program for the use of nuclear energy. In spite of disagreement on the policies here involved no one has asserted any violation of the First Amendment.

Secrecy regarding governmental operations has, however, spilled over into areas where justification on grounds of security does not exist at all or does not exist clearly. During World War II two or three departments dealing with top-secret matters were given sweeping authority to establish "nondisclosure" rules. In 1951 President Truman, by executive order, extended this right ("to classify" documents and information) to all departments and executive agencies. Without spelling out in detail the progress of this official policy, attention may be called to the setting up in the Department of Commerce of an Office of Strategic Information through which news with respect to the activities of the Department is filtered to the press. More recently, the Department of Defense restricted the flow of information about its activities by reducing the number of its public information personnel and by announcing that information would be withheld not only on grounds of security but also upon the basis of "whether the release or publication of material would constitute a constructive contribution to the primary mission of the Department of Defense." Newspapermen, congressional committees, and many others interested in civil liberties are seriously disturbed at the emergence in official Washington of a theory which puts the burden of proof upon those seeking information about operations of the government to show that the public interest would be served by its publication. Such policy invites concealment of information which has nothing to do with security but which might merely direct criticism against a department or agency.

There appear to be no legal penalties enforceable against newspapers which are able to get behind this secrecy blanket, but there are various informal types of discipline which government officers can bring to bear upon zealous reporters.

e. *Postal Censorship—Subversive Literature Imported from Abroad*

The major problem of postal censorship is dealt with *infra*, p. 30. Here it may merely be pointed out that in the interests of the national security subversive and dangerous printed matter may be barred from the country under criminal penalties and may be barred from the mails by punishing its distribution, by declaring the material to be nonmailable, or by denying it second-class mailing privileges. The civil liberty problems involved in these restraints upon the free flow of printed matter arise more from the procedures by which these rules are enforced than from the rules themselves.

2. Protection of the Administration of Justice —Contempt of Court

a. *Criticism of Courts by the Press*

Beginning in 1941 the Supreme Court has firmly established the doctrine that the right of the press to criticize courts and judges is protected by the First Amendment. Such criticism can be very virulent. (*Bridges* v. *California,* 314 U.S. 252, 1941; *Pennekamp* v. *Florida,* 328 U.S. 331, 1946; *Craig* v. *Harney,* 331 U.S. 367, 1947.) This doctrine of free criticism rests on the ground, stated by Justice Douglas in the Craig case, that "judges are supposed to be men of fortitude, able to thrive in a hardy climate," and that therefore only the most extraordinary and subversive press criticisms of courts or judicial proceedings can spell out a clear and present danger to the administration of justice.

Contempt of court through press criticism is, however, still possible. The problem involved is that of drawing the line between legitimate and illegitimate criticism. The problem will never be fully solved. In 1952 an irate judge in Georgia sentenced two newspaper editors to jail for refusing to print material, furnished by him, which was designed to answer published attacks upon the proceedings in his court. In the same year a trial judge in Virginia sought to punish a clergyman for public criticism of him.

In both cases state supreme courts reversed the convictions and upheld the right of criticism. *(McGill v. Georgia,* 209 Ga. 500, 1953; *Weston v. Commonwealth,* 195 Va. 175, 1953.)

b. *Contempt and the First Amendment*

A question of current importance is this: Can a man be punished for contempt either of court or of a legislative committee for refusing to testify on the ground that the questions asked violate his "right of silence" protected by the First Amendment? This problem has arisen mainly in connection with legislative committees investigating subversion. In several contempt cases now in the lower federal courts this issue is being raised.

c. *A Free Press and a Fair Trial*

An increasingly acute problem is that involving a conflict between two major civil liberties, freedom of the press and the right of an accused person to a trial in an atmosphere free from hysteria and prejudice. The problem has arisen out of the unrestrained and often unjustifiably lurid and inflammatory newspaper or radio reporting of pending or current prosecutions for crime. It is clear that this uninhibited reporting is protected, if not encouraged, by the Supreme Court's liberal doctrine regarding contempt by newspapers (see preceding page).

Current British practice contrasts sharply with our own. British courts permit no newspaper comment on current or pending criminal proceedings beyond the barest recital of the steps in the process. Between 1902 and 1949 thirteen editors or newspaper publishers were convicted of contempt. (Cases are summarized in appendix to opinion of Justice Frankfurter in *Maryland v. Baltimore Radio Show,*

338 U.S. 912, 921, 1950.) In 1949 the Lord Chief Justice fined the *London Daily Mirror* ten thousand pounds and sent its editor to jail for three months for the lurid reporting of the crimes of the so-called "English Bluebeard" then on trial for murder.

While the English rule will probably never be adopted in this country, American courts are increasingly alert to the seriousness of this problem. In 1952 the United States Circuit Court of Appeals granted a new trial to a federal collector of internal revenue in Boston, on the ground that after his indictment on criminal charges a congressional investigating committee conducted open hearings in Boston of such a nature as to inflame public opinion, thus creating a hostile atmosphere that in the judgment of the court would prevent a fair trial. *(Delaney* v. *United States,* 199 Fed. 2d 107, 1952.) In 1951 Justices Jackson and Frankfurter, concurring in a case granting four Florida Negroes a new trial on other grounds, emphasized vigorously that unrestrained press publicity regarding the case had created an atmosphere in the community in which a fair trial was impossible. *(Shepherd* v. *Florida,* 341 U.S. 50, 1951.) A trial court in Maryland sought to punish a broadcasting company for an inflammatory report that a man arrested for a brutal murder had confessed, had a long criminal record, and, upon being taken to the scene of the crime, had re-enacted it; the Court of Appeals of Maryland reversed the contempt conviction on the basis of the Supreme Court's liberal doctrine of contempt in Bridges, Pennekamp, and Craig. *(Maryland* v. *Baltimore Radio Show,* 193 Md. 300, 1949; certiorari denied, 338 U.S. 912, 1950.)

Responsible members of the newspaper and legal profession are acutely concerned because current hysteria is generating increasing conflicts between the rights of persons accused of crime and the rights of a free press. This warrants thorough study.

The problem discussed is not that which is involved in the exclusion of the press from a criminal trial on the grounds that the evidence is likely to be obscene. This was the issue in the recent Jelke trial in New York. The New York Court of Appeals granted a new trial to Jelke not on the ground that freedom of the press had been violated by the exclusion of reporters, but on the ground that the defendant's constitutional right to a "public" trial had been denied. *(People v. Jelke,* 308 N.Y. 56, 1954.)

d. *Protection of Newspaper Reporters and News Sources*

Can it be validly urged that freedom of the press creates the right of the newspaper reporter or publisher to refuse to disclose the sources of his news? The law has long protected from disclosure confidential communications between a lawyer and his client, as well as things said to a priest or clergyman under the seal of the confessional.

There is a sharp conflict of opinion on this issue. Substantial elements in the newspaper profession strongly urge that this immunity should be established. Judges and prosecutors usually oppose the idea. There is legislation in some states creating this immunity. Alabama has had such a statute since 1935.

3. PROTECTION OF PUBLIC MORALS AND DECENCY
—"CRIME, HORROR, SEX, AND BRUTALITY"

This is one of the traditionally proper restraints upon speech and press. It poses, as it always has and always will, important civil liberty problems. Current happenings are a bit paradoxical. Courts and legislatures are moving toward prudent and liberal laws and procedures in handling obscenity and related evils. At the same time there is a mounting demand in many quarters for drastic action against comic "books" and other literature thought to contribute to juvenile delinquency. One hundred million comics a month are sold in the United States. Juvenile delinquency, according to the findings of a Senate Committee, jumped 40 per cent between 1948 and 1953. Many people feel that these two facts are related, and they call for effective action.

a. *State and Local Laws Dealing with Obscene Books, Plays, and Movies*

The major activity in dealing with obscenity is on the state and local level. The protection of public morals is one of the basic purposes of the police power, and under our Constitution the police power rests with the states. Civil liberty problems here turn on (1) the standards by which the law defines what is obscene or otherwise objectionable; (2) the procedures by which a given book, play, or movie is held to conform or not conform to these standards. Three basic rights are involved in the solution of these problems: first, the right of the community to be protected against the undermining of public morality; second, the right to publish, circulate, and sell freely; third, the right of the public to read and to see.

(1) *Problems of standards and definitions.* While it is hard to define clearly and sharply what is obscene, there is common agreement that obscenity exists and should be dealt with by law, and there have been laws on the subject for a long time. The courts have held that the words "obscene," "lewd," and "lascivious" have acquired recognized legal meaning even though none of them can be

defined except by the use of synonyms which are equally general. Interpretations of the widest possible variety have been given to these terms over the years in decided cases.

Recent judicial interpretation has extended increasing protection to literature alleged to be obscene. There is growing judicial agreement that a book is not obscene merely because it contains scattered obscene passages, but that its character and impact as a whole shall be the test. Also, the book must be judged for its effect upon normal people rather than upon special groups peculiarly susceptible.

The courts insist that standards of obscenity, and so on, must have sharpness and clarity. Vague standards violate basic civil liberties. They violate due process of law, which requires that a crime be clearly enough defined so that a reasonable man may know when he is committing it. They also provide a cover for the banning of matter which the First Amendment might be held to protect.

This problem has been made concrete, although by no means entirely clear, by recent court decisions. In 1948 in the Winters case *(Winters* v. *New York,* 333 U.S. 507, 1948), the Supreme Court held void, on the ground of vagueness, a New York statute which prohibited publications made up principally of pictures or stories of "deeds of bloodshed, lust or crime." In the Burstyn case *(Burstyn* v. *Wilson,* 343 U.S. 495, 1952), involving the banning in New York of the film "The Miracle," a unanimous court held that due process was denied by subjecting motion picture films to prior censorship to determine whether or not they were "sacrilegious." The Court left open the question "whether a state may censor motion pictures under a clearly drawn statute designed and applied to prevent the showing of obscene films." Later the Supreme Court of Illinois upheld the banning of "The Miracle" on the ground of obscenity. (*American Civil Liberties Union* v. *City of Chicago*, 3 Ill. 2d 329, 1954.) The United States Supreme Court applied its ruling in the Burstyn case to strike down a New York ban on a motion picture on the ground that "it would tend to corrupt morals" and an Ohio ban "on account of being harmful." (*Commercial Pictures Corp.* v. *Regents of University of State of New York, Superior Films, Inc.* v. *Department of Education of Ohio*, 346 U.S. 587, 1954.) Those presently crusading against what they regard as objectionable literature and movies are somewhat distraught by these decisions. Several state legislatures have been struggling to enact laws which would deal effectively with the abuses of those comic books considered to be below a reasonable moral standard. The states confront a very difficult problem, since ragbag definitions made up of terms like "brutality," "depravity," and "horror" seem unlikely to be upheld by the courts.

(2) *Enforcement methods and procedures.* Satisfactorily clear definitions and standards will not alone protect civil liberties in this area. Serious abuses arise in connection with the methods and procedures by which the standards of obscenity and so forth are applied to specific cases. Four general procedures have emerged:

The first is punishment after publication. Almost every state, and many local governments, punish the publication, distribution, and sale of obscene matter. People are not prevented from such publishing, distributing, and selling, but are punished later if they are guilty of it. This method most effectively protects civil liberties. It avoids the dangers inherent in prior censorship and it immediately brings all crucial issues into a court of law. The burden of proving violation of law rests here, as in all criminal cases, upon the state.

The second method is administrative control. This is not very common. It involves the seizure and confiscation of obscene matter under the authority of executive or administrative officers or boards, and it may also involve revocation of the licenses to sell publications commonly required of news venders. The rulings of such administrative authorities cannot legally be made final, but it rests with those subject to such authority to seek redress in the courts.

The third method may be described as informal government action—a realistic rather than a legal definition. This is very common and is on the increase. Lists of alleged obscene books and magazines frequently put together by outside crusading groups (though sometimes by the police themselves) are circulated by the police to news sellers or bookstores, with either threats or suggestions that, unless books on the list are withdrawn, dire and frequently undefined consequences will ensue. The threat of undesirable publicity, possible loss of good will, and the fear of prosecution are set in motion. Frequently blacklisted books are offensive only to minority groups, and their suppression is by no means clearly in the public interest. Outside pressures are frequently so dominant in the compiling of these lists as to convert the whole procedure into a form of private censorship. This type of activity is illustrated by the case of Youngstown, Ohio, in which the chief of police developed a list of books and magazines finally reaching 443 and threatened newsdealers and booksellers with jail if the publications were not withdrawn; in 1953 a United

States district court in Ohio put an end to this arbitrary censorship. *(New American Library of World Literature, Inc.* v. *Allen,* 114 Fed. Supp. 823, 1953.)

I have called this "informal" governmental action, because in many cases in which it goes on there is no law or authority under which the threat resorted to could be backed up. Needed sanctions, however, are often provided by local public opinion which supports the action of the police.

It has been suggested that abridgments by police officers of First Amendment rights could be dealt with by prosecuting the officers under the Civil Rights Act, which forbids anyone "under color of law" to deny or abridge such rights. It is most unlikely that such action will be taken or would succeed if it were.

The fourth and most controversial procedure is that of prior censorship. Since the Supreme Court's decision in *Near* v. *Minnesota* in 1931, (283 U.S. 697) books, magazines, and newspapers are protected against prior censorship. The Court made plain in that case that this was the particular kind of restriction of freedom of the press which the First Amendment was designed to prevent.

With regard, however, to movies, shows, and the theater, prior censorship has long prevailed. None of the cases holding void the banning of particular motion pictures by boards of censorship has ruled that prior censorship of films is invalid in all cases. The question is still open whether the prior censorship of motion pictures under a clearly defined standard of obscenity will be upheld.

The problem may become academic, for prior censorship seems to be on its way out. In 1954 it was held unconstitutional in Ohio (*R.K.O. Pictures* v. *Department of*

Education, 162 Ohio 263, following the Burstyn rule); in 1955 after thirty-eight years it was repealed by the Kansas legislature. Contrary to a popular impression that it exists widely, there are only five states in the Union which require the prior censorship and licensing of motion pictures, although such censorship prevails in many cities. Newsreels are not censored in any state in the Union. There is some current demand for the prior censorship of comic books on the ground that they present a sufficiently unique and dangerous threat to warrant taking them out from under the rule of the Near case, but these demands seem likely to fail.

Prior censorship has always been regarded as the most dangerous denial of First Amendment rights, not only because it places the writer, publisher, and bookseller at the mercy of the censor, but because by its operation it prevents the public from knowing what is being banned and thus makes impossible the creation of an informed public opinion in the matter. Statements made by censors that "the people do not know what is bad for them" rest upon more false assumptions than can be set out here.

States may not censor radio and television at all. In 1950 a federal court of appeals, in the Dumont Laboratories case *(Dumont Laboratories* v. *Carroll,* 184 Fed. 2d 153, 1950), so held on the ground that radio and television, as parts of interstate commerce, must be kept free from state control. The Supreme Court denied certiorari. *(Carroll* v. *Dumont Laboratories,* 340 U.S. 929, 1951.)

The state censorship of schoolbooks and school libraries will be dealt with in connection with academic freedom. (*Infra,* p. 85.) Censorship of books in public libraries can probably be defended on legal grounds on the basis of the public ownership of such libraries.

In this whole problem of censorship the competence and caliber of the censor looms up as an important factor. His rulings, if arbitrary, may be nullified by the courts, but in too many cases the people subject to his rulings cannot afford judicial redress. Experience unhappily proves that the job of the censor often does not attract persons of very high capacity.

b. *Federal Censorship of Obscenity*

The national government has no broad police power to protect the morals of the country. It can, however, deal with the problems of obscenity through certain of its delegated powers.

(1) Congress controls what may be imported into the United States. The importation of obscene pictures has been forbidden since 1842, and of obscene literature since 1890. In recent years the earlier clumsy enforcement of this censorship by customs officials has been vastly improved by calling in the expert advice of Mr. Huntington Cairns, later the secretary of the National Gallery of Art, to help determine whether particular books or pictures ought to be excluded.

(2) The postal laws forbid circulation through the mails of obscene literature, pictures, and contraceptive articles and information. A statute of 1950 goes much further. It authorizes the Postmaster General to cut off all mail to a person who mails obscene matter, which amounts to putting him out of business—a very different thing from refusing to circulate only his obscene literature or pictures. A recent decision in the Court of Appeals of the District of Columbia has limited this power. (See *infra*, p. 34.) Postal censorship poses very important civil liberty prob-

lems, and it will be dealt with in a separate section. *(Infra,* p. 30.)

(3) Congress has forbidden the shipping in interstate commerce of much the same type of obscene and objectionable matter which it has barred from the mails. Violations of the postal laws are easier to discover than unlawful shipments in interstate commerce because of the administrative machinery provided by the post office itself.

(4) The District of Columbia is under the direct authority of Congress, and the power of Congress to deal with obscene and other objectionable publications in the District is the same as that of any state or city.

(5) Radio and television stations operate under licenses issued by the Federal Communications Commission. The stations do not own the wave lengths which they use. The Federal Communications Act forbids the Federal Communications Commission to exercise censorship over programs. The Commission may, however, refuse to renew the license of, or may cancel the license of, radio and television stations found to be operating contrary to the public interest. As will be seen later on *(infra,* pp. 39, 44), the problem of censorship in radio and television is somewhat unique. Self-censorship by the broadcasting industry itself plus the informal censorship of public opinion, which is quick to be offended, have pretty well prevented the question of the exercise of legal censorship from arising.

4. Protection of Private Interests against Libel and Slander

a. *Libel or Slander of Individuals*

The man who defames another person does not enjoy the constitutional protection of speech and press in so doing. Where the matters discussed are not of public concern, the harm resulting to the individual outweighs any public interest.

The chief civil liberty problem connected with libel and slander *per se* is whether in American courts the remedy available to the defamed person is adequate. Leaving out of account the rare cases of criminal libel, the remedy is confined to money damages awarded in a civil suit. Threatened libel may not be enjoined. The victim must await publication of the libel and then collect damages if he can. For some years British courts have been somewhat cautiously issuing injunctions in libel cases.

The issue here is debatable. Against the greater protection of the individual must be put the dangers to freedom of expression in what amounts to judicial prior censorship.

The law of libel and slander dealing with defamation by private persons is complex. It is much more complex in its application to newspaper services, radio, and television. Here legal liability may often come to rest upon those not personally responsible for the defamation. Injustices exist here which call for study, but the complexity of the problem precludes analysis of it here.

In the area of the public discussion of public affairs, several important problems connected with libel have emerged. The protection of individuals against libel must not stifle the full and fair discussion of public affairs. Three problems arise in this connection:

(1) *Privileged statements.* It has long been recognized that public officers engaged in the management of public affairs must be allowed to speak more freely with regard to personal misconduct, criminality, or abuses of public trust by others than would be the case were they private

citizens. Thus, what is said by the prosecutor or by witnesses in a court of law, or in the hearings of legislative committees, or before other government investigating agencies, is protected by "privilege," and libel actions may not be based on such statements.

Fair and accurate newspaper comments made without malice and based upon such public records is also "privileged." The impact of this rule of privilege upon civil liberties is often acute.

(2) *Congressional immunity.* A special phase of the "doctrine of privilege" is the rule of legislative immunity. This very old rule was embodied in the English Bill of Rights of 1689. The protection of members of legislative bodies from libel actions based upon speeches made in official debate is essential. Not to do so would stifle free legislative discussion. The members of every American legislature enjoy this immunity.

Civil liberties are frequently abridged under this rule of congressional immunity. This has been especially true in the management of congressional committee hearings. Irresponsible "name-dropping" either by Congressmen or by witnesses in the recital of Communist associations may seriously damage innocent persons. And on the floor of both houses of Congress, individuals have been accused of crime, treason, or disloyalty. None of these persons has any remedy since libel actions are barred.

The resulting injustices have been widely discussed and the following proposals have been made:

(a) Discipline by the Senate or House of members guilty of these abuses.

(b) A statute allowing damage suits to be brought in federal court by an injured person either against the United States or against either house.

(c) A statute permitting a person slandered on the floor of either house, or perhaps before a congressional committee, to print a reply in the *Congressional Record*.

(d) A statute limiting the immunity of congressmen to statements made within the chamber of either house. Immunity would not extend to matter in the Appendix of the *Congressional Record* or in "Extension of Remarks."

(e) A constitutional amendment limiting immunity to things said in Congress about the conduct of public officers or of those acting under government authority or of those handling public money. Immunity would not extend to statements about private persons.

(3) *Fair comment.* Public officials may themselves be defamed, and the laws of libel deal with this problem through the doctrine of "fair comment." This doctrine assumes that the reputation and conduct of a public official are matters of public concern and often justify criticisms and attacks upon him which might be libelous if directed against a private citizen. Fair comment must be based on facts truly stated. One needs only to follow the daily press to be aware of the extent to which persons in public life may be reviled and accused of misconduct without having recourse to libel action.

In 1952 an unsuccessful attempt was made in Louisiana to prosecute five newspapermen for criminal libel for the criticism of public officials.

b. *Some Proposals for Dealing with Current Problems Connected with Libel*

It is generally agreed that the existing laws of libel do not give full protection to persons who are defamed. Methods have been discussed for increasing this protection. The principal ones are as follows:

(1) In a number of states the voluntary publication of a retraction of a libel has been given the legal effect of excusing the publisher from punitive damages, though he is still liable for actual damage resulting from the libel.

(2) A person who has published a libel should be compelled to publish a corrected statement or a retraction.

(3) Right of reply. In France and Germany persons who can show damage resulting from newspaper libels must promptly be allowed equal space to answer the defamatory statements.

c. *Group Libel—Antihate Legislation*

The problems presented by hate propaganda have increased over the past two or three decades. Public vilification of racial or religious groups makes difficult the orderly and tolerant handling of problems of policy in a democratic state and encourages discrimination and violations of civil rights.

Laws to deal with these abuses have been given the label, "group libel laws." "Group libel" is a catch-all phrase used to include a wide range of critical comment that particular groups find objectionable. In essence, a group libel statute is a law by which those who publish or circulate statements which defame racial and religious groups are made legally responsible for their actions. This extends the law of libel from the individual to the group. There are three types of group libel legislation:

(1) *Federal legislation*. This is based on the commerce and postal powers of Congress. Ever since 1935, when Representative Samuel Dickstein first sought to make pro-Axis propaganda (much of which was anti-Semitic) nonmailable, bills have been introduced in every Congress barring from

the mails and from the channels of interstate commerce this kind of defamatory material. One was introduced in 1955. No such proposal has ever been reported from committee, and only once did such a bill reach the hearing stage.

(2) *State laws aimed specifically at group libel.* Illinois in 1917 passed an antihate law forbidding the exhibition of any play, drama, or sketch which exposes citizens of any race, color, creed, or religion to contempt, derision, or obloquy. Designed as a basis for censoring motion pictures, the law became in 1941 and 1942 a weapon for harassing those Jehovah's Witnesses who indulge in sharp attacks upon the Catholic Church.

New Jersey in 1935 passed an act directed primarily against the German-American Bund. The Act punished speeches or statements inciting, promoting, or advocating hostility against any group (residing in the state) because of race, color, or religion. The act was invalidated in part, and the rest became ineffective.

Indiana in 1947 passed a law aimed at the Ku Klux Klan. The law made illegal both conspiracies for the purpose of disseminating hatred and also "the actual dissemination of hatred" tending to cause breaches of the peace, interference with traffic, or the denial of civil or constitutional rights. Although it was invoked once, there has been no successful prosecution under it.

(3) *State laws extending traditional libel laws to racial and religious groups.* Massachusetts does this explicitly, while in other states libel legislation is broad enough to make possible suits for group defamation.

In April of 1952 the Supreme Court handed down its five-to-four decision in *Beauharnais* v. *Illinois.* (343 U.S.

250, 1952.) Beauharnais had been convicted of violating the Illinois antihate law of 1917 after he distributed a disgusting anti-Negro tirade calling for the continuation of segregated housing in Chicago. The Supreme Court stated that the Act of 1917 had been construed by the Illinois courts in the Beauharnais case not as an exercise of the police power but as an extension of the law of criminal libel. It was therefore constitutional, because libelous utterances are not protected by the First Amendment.

Some minority groups, mainly those which are targets of group libel, still favor these laws. Other groups, those more broadly interested in civil liberties, either oppose them or are increasingly doubtful. In 1947 the President's Committee on Civil Rights declined to support group libel legislation. This is also the position of the American Civil Liberties Union. The American Jewish Congress, originally strongly favorable, is no longer pushing this program. The reasons seem to be, first, some falling off in the stream of hate-literature; second, increasing doubts as to the effectiveness of such laws; and third, serious misgivings that these new legal restraints on speech and press may actually result in dangerous limitations on free public discussion. There is a growing feeling that the abuses can be better dealt with by other methods.

d. *The Right of Privacy*

The question crops up occasionally whether there is a civil liberty which can be called the right of privacy. This of course is not to be confused with that right of privacy which is protected against unreasonable searches and seizures, a problem that will be dealt with elsewhere. *(Infra,* p. 135.)

The common law did not recognize a right of privacy.

In 1890 Louis D. Brandeis and an associate published in the *Harvard Law Review* an article entitled "Right to Privacy," urging that such a right does exist in justice and that it should be protected in the judicial interpretation of the law.

In the absence of judge-made law protecting the right to privacy, the New York legislature in 1903 extended protection to any person whose name or property is used for trade or advertising purposes without his consent in writing. Three other states follow the New York rule without any special statute. The New York Act did not accomplish the purpose aimed at and, in fact, left in its wake a long line of decisions and judgments never anticipated and often not very desirable.

There seems to be no current demand for action with respect to the right of privacy.

5. Protection against Speeches and Publications Alleged to Be Nuisances

Governmental restrictions upon speech and press are imposed by state and local governments in the exercise of their police powers under which they may abate nuisances and restrain those who threaten the safety, order, and convenience of the community. While these police regulations are usually not intended as restraints upon First Amendment rights, they nevertheless fall upon people who wish to make speeches, operate sound trucks, distribute literature, or canvass from house to house. These conflicts of interest pose difficult, though somewhat limited, free speech and press problems, which concern the following:

a. *Speeches in Public Places*

The problem of restrictions on speeches or parades in public places (streets or parks) is not to be confused with the broad problem of freedom of assembly. The factors which are involved are the interest which the public has in preventing traffic obstruction, the property interest of the city in its streets or parks, and over against these the long-standing tradition that these public places are the normal ones for making speeches and conducting parades. The lines must be carefully drawn here.

b. *Licenses for Speeches*

Could the problem be solved by issuing licenses (with nominal fees) or by the registration of those who wish to make speeches in public? Civil liberty issues here turn on the kind of discretion given to local officials to grant or withhold such licenses. The problems connected with religious meetings are dealt with elsewhere. (*Infra*, p. 94.)

c. *Sound Trucks*

The difficult problems posed by sound trucks have resulted in confusing and somewhat conflicting court decisions. Some restraints are clearly valid, while a total ban is clearly invalid.

d. *Distribution of Literature on Streets and to Homes*

Regulations of persons selling or distributing literature on the streets or from house to house present another confusing problem. Protection against dubious itinerant peddlers is clearly desirable, but such protection could provide officials with power to exercise censorship and restrict freedom of the press. There is greater authority to control the distribution of secular than of religious literature, as will appear later. (*Infra*, p. 94.)

6. Assurance of the Political Neutrality and Loyalty of Public Employees

a. *The Hatch Act and the "Little Hatch Acts"*

The political activity of civil servants has long posed a problem. The Hatch Act, passed in 1939, forbids the officers and employees in the executive branch of the federal government (with certain exceptions at the top) to take an active part in political management or in political campaigns. There is a substantial amount of state and local legislation of the same sort. In sustaining the Hatch Act against the charge that it violated the First Amendment, the Supreme Court stated that political activity of federal employees could reasonably be regarded as an interference with the efficiency of the public service. It said also that political activity tends to damage public confidence in the civil service, which, in the public mind, should be neutral. These public interests were deemed sufficient to justify the sharp curtailment of the freedom of speech and press of those who work for the government. *(United Public Workers v. Mitchell,* 330 U.S. 75, 1947.)

There is also present here the question of "employer-employee" relationship in government and the doctrine that public employment is a privilege and not a right. It was in construing a Massachusetts city ordinance of the Hatch Act variety that Justice Holmes, then on the supreme court of the state, uttered his familiar comment, "The petitioner may have a constitutional right to talk politics, but he has no constitutional right to be a policeman." *(McAuliffe v. New Bedford,* 155 Mass. 216, 1892.)

While the Holmes epigram seems to spell absolute discretion in the government in dealing with its employees, the Supreme Court, in upholding the Hatch Act (see above), agreed readily that Congress could not validly "enact a regulation providing that no Republican, Jew or Negro shall be appointed to federal office, or that no federal employee shall attend Mass or take any active part in missionary work."

The civil liberty problems posed here turn first on the basic philosophy of the legislation. Is the public interest which is protected great enough to justify this invasion of First Amendment rights? France and Britain impose much less rigorous restraints. Second, there is the issue of the fairness with which these laws are enforced. Instances of arbitrary or discriminatory action sometimes come to light.

b. *Loyalty-Security Requirements*

These are later dealt with (*infra*, p. 166) more fully. Congress, presidents, and attorneys general all deny that loyalty-security programs, designed to keep the public service free from subversives, are intended to impose or do impose restraints on the First Amendment rights of public servants. However, federal inquiry into what a public employee reads, sees, publishes, and so on—an inquiry made in an effort to discover if he has such possibly unorthodox political or economic views as to make his continued employment not "clearly consistent with the interests of the national security" (see present security order)—is bound to restrain public employees from the kind of speaking or writing which would make them "controversial" figures.

c. *Censorship of Official Speech, and Speech in the Armed Services*

This is not the problem of the release of information to the public which was discussed above. (*Supra*, p. 5.)

No question of civil liberty is involved in requiring a government officer to keep his mouth shut about his official business. There are no First Amendment rights here.

Much more doubtful are the policies of censorship in the armed services, policies designed not to safeguard secret information or the national security but to quarantine armed services personnel against dangerous or doubtful influences. This policy was highlighted recently by the refusal of West Point and Annapolis to allow their boys to debate the "controversial" question of our recognition of Red China. The same policy is followed in the screening of books in post libraries and the reading matter available to men in the armed services. Since the person involved is "captive" in the sense of being under rigid discipline, the questions raised here are questions of policy rather than of legal right.

7. Postal Censorship and Allied Problems—First Amendment Rights Reduced to "Privileges"

There has come to be embedded in our law the rather disturbing doctrine that when, in exercising First Amendment rights, one uses media of communication which are owned or directed by the government these rights become "privileges" to be enjoyed pretty much on the government's own terms.

There is a basic plausibility to this. The ownership of facilities for communication would seem to give to the owner the right to say by whom and how they are to be used. Certainly the right of a private owner to control his own property, wisely or unwisely, is, with some necessary exceptions, freely recognized.

Public ownership, however, differs sharply from private ownership. Not only is the government limited by constitutional restraints, but what we speak of as its ownership is in the nature of a trusteeship for the people. In spite of these obvious differences, the doctrine that the use of government-owned facilities is a privilege still persists, and a serious current threat to freedom of speech and press is government control exercised on this "privilege" theory. The problems involved vary with the nature of the facility and may be discussed briefly on that basis.

a. *Postal Censorship*

Postal censorship, as we have seen (*supra,* p. 18), is one of the ways by which we combat obscenity. It poses, however, unique problems affecting First Amendment rights in general. Postal censorship is currently undergoing some changes; important ones have come about since the close of World War II, and others seem to be in the offing. Present problems and developments in the field have meaning only against some background.

(1) *Postal censorship in capsule form at the close of World War II.* The basic doctrine that the use of the mails is a privilege has long been established. The doctrine means that the government does us a favor in carrying the mails (especially second-class mail) and has therefore broader power over the mails than it would otherwise have.

The government's control over the use of the mail is comprised in four legal approaches: First, Congress has forbidden, under criminal penalties, the shipment through the mails of a long list of things, including dead animals, explosives, matter with insufficient postage, obscene and seditious matter, matter tending to incite arson, murder and assassination, and fraudulent matter. Second, Congress has forbidden the Post Office Department to carry or deliver any of this nonmailable matter. Third, Congress has authorized the Postmaster General to stop all incoming mail addressed to persons conducting a fraud (this was after the end of World War II) or using a fictitious name or address. Fourth, Congress has divided mail matter into four classes, depending largely upon its subject matter, and has authorized the Postmaster General to administer these classifications.

While the first of these approaches involves criminal prosecution in the courts, the last three are administered directly by the Post Office Department, and it is here that the Postmaster General derives his powers of censorship. The process works as follows:

First, the Postmaster General may decide that something is obscene, seditious, or otherwise nonmailable, and refuse to carry or deliver it. There is no procedure required by statute for this determination, and in practice it is made by the postmaster who is asked to receive the matter for mailing. The Circuit Court of Appeals held in the *Masses* case *(Masses Publishing Co. v. Patten,* 245 Fed. 102, 1917) that the postmaster's interpretation must stand unless clearly wrong, and this decision has been generally followed.

Second, the Postmaster General may revoke the second-class mailing privileges of publications enjoying them. The statute requires a hearing for this action since heavy financial interests are at stake, but there has been no substantial judicial review of revocation orders on the merits. In the *Milwaukee Leader* case in 1921 *(Milwaukee Social Democratic Publishing Co. v. Burleson,* 255 U.S. 407, 1921), the Supreme Court upheld the revocation of the second-class mailing privilege of a socialist newspaper on the ground that several issues had contained nonmailable material. Future issues of the publication must be mailed at the higher postal rates until the Postmaster General is convinced that no nonmailable material will appear. This of course amounts to prior censorship, although the procedures involved in revoking the privilege guarantee due process of law.

Third, the Postmaster General may, "on evidence satisfactory to him" that a person is conducting a fraud (or selling obscene matter), cut off incoming mail. Despite the fact that this action would effectively put a person or company out of business, no hearing was required by statute and only an informal and somewhat unsatisfactory hearing was given in such cases. The only actual case here involving First Amendment rights concerned an allegedly religious group using the mails in connection with a faith-healing scheme. *(United States* v. *Ballard,* 322 U.S. 78, 1944.)

(2) *A decade of changes in postal censorship.* During the last ten years court decisions have given increasing protection to First Amendment rights against censorship by the Post Office. The *Esquire* case *(Hannegan* v. *Esquire, Inc.,* 327 U.S. 146, 1946) denied the right of the Postmaster General, claimed under the Classification Act, to deny second-class privileges to a periodical unless in his judgment it "contributes to the public good and the public welfare." The case continued in force the old rule that publications held to be "nonmailable" may be denied second-class privileges; at the same time it cast some doubt on the "privilege" doctrine. The Supreme Court said that "grave constitutional questions are immediately raised once it is said that the use of the mails is a privilege which may be extended or withheld on any grounds whatsoever."

The extent of the power over publications given the Postmaster General by the fraud statutes came before the Supreme Court in a fraud order case in 1948. *(Donaldson v. Read Magazine,* 333 U.S. 178, 1948.) On the ground that one of the puzzles published in *Facts* magazine was fraudulent, the Postmaster General cut off all mail addressed to its editors, who were also editors of *Read.* The right to "virtually put both magazines out of business" was argued twice before the Court, but before the second argument the Postmaster General modified his order, limiting it to the contest editor of the offending puzzle. The Court agreed that the puzzle was fraudulent, but it emphasized in a dictum that the Postmaster General not only had the power "but he had the duty" so to reduce the scope of the order. "The purpose of mail fraud orders," it said, "is not punishment but prevention of future injury to the public." In 1950 Congress extended this power to cut off incoming mail to persons selling obscenity, and in 1954 the Post Office Department cut off the incoming mail of a nudist publication on the ground that one of its issues was obscene. In *Summerfield* v. *Sunshine Book Company* (221 Fed. 2d 42, 1954) the Court of Appeals in the District of Columbia reversed the order on the ground that it would obstruct the publication of future issues which might not be obscene. This barring of future issues, said the court, raises grave constitutional questions. The Supreme Court declined to review the case. (349 U.S. 921, 1955.)

The courts have also dealt with Post Office procedures. In cases revoking second-class mailing privileges, hearings have always been required by statute; and the nature of these hearings has been much improved after the Attorney General's Committee on Administrative Procedure made its report in 1940. The Administrative Procedure Act of

1946 sets up a procedural code for the conduct of *all* hearings required by statute to be held by any administrative agency of the government. There could be no doubt that this Act applied automatically to the second-class mailing privilege cases, and the Post Office Department immediately accepted this and applied the new procedures.

The problem remained, however, whether the Administrative Procedure Act applied to cases of exclusion from the mails. At first it seemed not. By its own language the Administrative Procedure Act applies "wherever hearings are required by statute," and the postal statutes required no hearings in exclusion cases, even though the Department had been holding them voluntarily. In 1948 the solicitor of the Post Office Department ruled that the Administrative Procedure Act does not apply to exclusion cases, but at the same time the Department's voluntary hearing procedures were much improved. It may be noted that in 1945, before the Administrative Procedure Act, the Court of Appeals of the District of Columbia had held that due process of law requires notice and hearing before books on sex can be barred from the mails. (*Walker* v. *Popenoe,* 149 Fed. 2d 511, 1945.) The case was not appealed. In 1950, however, in *Wong Yang Sung* v. *McGrath* (339 U.S. 33), a deportation case, the Supreme Court held that the Administrative Procedure Act applies wherever a hearing is required by statute or *wherever a hearing is required by due process of law.* It held that, according to due process, Wong Yang Sung could not be deported without a hearing. In the face of this decision the Post Office after some hesitation capitulated and set about applying the Administrative Procedure Act to its exclusion cases. This represents a substantial gain in fair procedures.

(3) *Continuing problems in postal censorship.* The gains mentioned above fall short of solving postal censorship problems. Three such problems remain for consideration and solution:

First is the problem of *who* is to determine what is obscene or otherwise nonmailable. Under present laws this is the Postmaster General, a man whose chief qualifications are usually that he successfully managed the President's campaign for election. This is no reflection on his possible high qualities, but it would seem that if there is to be censorship the judgment of informed and somewhat expert persons should be brought into the process. In the procedure established by the Treasury, an expert consultant gives advice on borderline cases when the importation of books and pictures is questioned.

A second important issue is that of the range of judicial review of censorship decisions. At present, judicial review is kept to the minimum. The courts offer the best hope of building up sound censorship standards, as they have been doing over the years in obscenity cases. The argument that judicial review in this area would overburden the courts does not seem sound, since a relatively limited number of borderline cases would in practice come before the courts.

In the third place, should the judicial doctrine of "privilege" be abandoned or sharply modified? In other areas of the law this has already occurred. Towns and cities are not allowed to plead their ownership of streets and public parks as a basis for denying First Amendment rights in the distribution of literature or the holding of public meetings. In *Tucker* v. *Texas* (326 U.S. 517, 1946) the Supreme Court held that a federally owned village built and managed by the Federal Public Housing Authority could not, on the basis of such proprietorship, bar the distribution of religious literature.

The privilege doctrine seems unsound in the face of the doctrine of "unconstitutional conditions." As far back as 1910 the Supreme Court announced that it is a denial of due process of law for a state to require a foreign corporation, as the price of enjoying a privilege which may be withheld, to give up a constitutional right. *(Western Union Tel. Co. v. Kansas,* 216 U.S. 1, 1910.) This doctrine has appeared in numerous cases. It is clearly stated by Judge Edgerton in his dissent in *Bailey* v. *Richardson* (182 Fed. 2d 46, 1950) in dealing with the privilege of holding federal office. The idea that postal services are favors, and favors which the government does not have to extend, does not jibe with the fact that the Post Office is a legal monopoly and that if the government does not carry the mail it does not get carried. Finally, it should be kept in mind that the purpose of postal service, and especially second-class mailing privileges, is not to create privileges or subsidies but to further the national interest by increasing the free flow of printed matter.

Controversy has arisen over the censorship by the Post Office (and Customs Bureau) of "foreign propaganda"— printed matter from Russia, Red China, and sometimes other countries. The Post Office will deliver these newspapers and other publications *(Pravda, Izvestia)* to universities, libraries, certain public officials, but not to private individuals generally. The authority for this action is the Foreign Agents Registration Act, but it has been strongly urged that the statute does not give the Post Office power summarily to exclude this propaganda material. The courts have not yet passed on the issue.

b. *Censorship by Customs Authorities of Imported Literature*

The authority to bar the importation of printed matter and pictures also rests upon the doctrine that such importation is a privilege and not a right. In fact, the doctrine has more force here than in connection with the Post Office. Congress has barred obscene pictures from the country since 1842, and obscene literature since 1890. In the enforcement of these laws, censorship for many years was exercised by the men who inspect your luggage in the customs shed—a situation very like allowing the policeman on the beat to censor literature on the newsstand. The Treasury Department was frequently the object of ridicule as a result of the inept handling of these difficult problems.

In 1940 Congress made an important change by distinguishing between ordinary literature and "so-called classics or the books of recognized and established literary and scientific merit—imported for non-commercial purposes." At the same time the final authority to determine issues of obscenity under the Customs Act was given to the federal courts.

In 1934, after losing his case in the courts to bar *Ulysses* from importation *(United States v. One Book Entitled Ulysses,* 72 Fed. 2d 705, 1934), Secretary Morgenthau appointed Mr. Huntington Cairns, a lawyer and also an art connoisseur, as special legal advisor to the Treasury. Where books are actually excluded by lesser officials, he has been brought in to give his judgment on the issue. Since his appointment no cases have gone to the courts. This seems to be a reasonable way to deal with this difficult problem and one which might be extended to other parts of the government where censorship is carried on.

c. *Radio and Television*

The problems of freedom of expression over radio and television are unique. The radio industry came to the federal government almost on its knees and asked to be regulated. The core of the problem is that while the government owns the radio and television wave lengths (just as it owns the facilities for the distribution of mail) there are not enough wave lengths to go around. The government can place no limit upon the number of speeches a man can make or the number of papers or pamphlets he can print; but there are definite limits to the number of possible radio and television stations and to the number of broadcasting hours in any day. The result is that Congress, through the Federal Communications Commission, retains a range of control over radio and television which would be quite unthinkable in respect to speech and press generally.

Congressional policy in regard to radio and television has two major elements in it: (1) direct censorship and (2) licensing, with its problem of indirect censorship. The policy is stated in congressional statutes and is administered by the Federal Communications Commission. These and other issues are discussed below:

(1) *Direct censorship.* No censorship powers are given to the Federal Communications Commission. In fact, Congress has explicitly forbidden such censorship. This means that the Federal Communications Commission may not censor any program in advance of broadcast and may not issue any "cease and desist" order. The Criminal Code itself makes the broadcasting of obscenity and other objectional matter a penal offense, but these statutes are enforced by the Department of Justice, not the Federal

Communications Commission. As we shall see later on (*infra,* p. 44), the industry is constantly under pressure from public opinion to censor its programs.

Congress could grant powers of censorship to the Federal Communications Commission as it has granted them to the Postmaster General. Occasionally proposals are made for doing this. It has, for example, been proposed in Congress that the equal-time privilege guaranteed by statute to political candidates shall be denied to persons convicted of subversive activity and to members of subversive organizations. There is a steady stream of proposals to ban lotteries, obscene matter, liquor and gambling advertisements, and other material from the air. In 1953 a House committee studied this whole problem and reported against establishing such censorship.

(2) *Licensing.* The Federal Communications Commission grants licenses "in the public interest, convenience and necessity," and all licenses must be renewed periodically. "The air belongs to the public, and not to the radio industry." Wayne Coy, former chairman of the Federal Communications Commission, has stated, "Congress intended that radio stations shall not be used for the private interests, whims, or caprices of the particular persons who have been granted licenses."

In determining (under generous judicial supervision) whether stations have operated, or will operate, in the "public interest," the Federal Communications Commission has clearly very broad authority over the actual broadcasting output. It can rescind a license after elaborate administrative procedures and for sufficient grounds, and it can refuse to renew a license. This clearly spells out an indirect form of control that, while it is not actual censorship, is nonetheless potent. In actual practice, casually expressed desires of Federal Communications Commission members tend to be followed by the networks. There are those, however, who feel that the Federal Communications Commission, through timidity or inertia, has failed to use its licensing powers to secure adequate protection of the "public interest, convenience and necessity" in radio and television. This broad power raises problems concerning several matters:

(a) *Obscenity.* It is clear that, while the Federal Communications Commission may not censor programs for obscenity, it may deny a license to a station which has broadcast objectionable matter. Professor Kenneth Davis tells us: "When intonations of Mae West in a broadcast were thought obscene, the Chairman of the Commission wrote the president of the network, warning all stations carrying the program that the incident would be considered with their renewal applications." *(Administrative Law,* pp. 139 ff.)

(b) *"Editorializing."* The problem of "editorializing" on the air remains a controversial one. In 1941 in the so-called "Mayflower decision" the Federal Communications Commission renewed the license of a station which had been steadily broadcasting the political views of the station owner, but it warned that this "editorializing" must cease. This rule does not apply to commentators hired either by the station or by the sponsors. The principle that a radio station cannot be used to further the political beliefs of the licensee was attacked by the industry as a denial of First Amendment rights. In 1948, after elaborate public hearings, the Commission relaxed the restriction on editorializing but at the same time announced that the privilege must not be used for one-sided or partisan presentation of controversial issues and that a "balanced presentation" was required. No cases have arisen under the new rule.

(c) *Political broadcasts.* The statute explicitly forbids censorship of political broadcasts, and the Federal Communications Commission has rigidly enforced this rule against stations which have sought to violate it. In 1953 WABD canceled a broadcast by an avowed Communist, stating, "We did not think it in the public interest to provide time to Communists for the espousal of Communist doctrine." It has not been judicially determined whether such action violates the statute.

The Act also requires that equal time on the air be given to political candidates. This means a "legally qualified candidate," and the right is a personal one. It does not extend to political parties as such or to those who make speeches in behalf of candidates. Many problems of justice and fair play arise in the administration of this rule. So far the question whether a member of the Communist Party may be a "legally qualified candidate" is determined by state law. Whether, under the Communist Control Act, a Communist can be a candidate has not yet been decided.

(d) *Allocation of time.* There is a mounting demand that fixed allotments of time on the air be devoted to educational programs. The Federal Communications Commission could probably compel reasonable allocations for this purpose. That a serious free speech problem lurks in such a program is shown by the proposals of those who wish to sponsor educational programs that broadcasts for this purpose shall not present "controversial matters." Serious censorship implications are implicit in any such ban.

In 1946 the Federal Communications Commission issued

its famous Blue Book dealing with "the public service responsibility of broadcasters." It set forth four factors relating broadly to the public interest which the Federal Communications Commission said it intended to consider when renewing stations' licenses. The Blue Book was widely attacked by the industry as an attempt to control programing and consequently as an invasion of First Amendment rights. No station appears to have been denied a license for any violation of the programing standards set out in the Blue Book.

The American Civil Liberties Union filed a complaint with the Federal Communications Commission against the renewal of the license of networks alleged to engage in blacklisting. The Federal Communications Commission has taken no action.

(3) *Defamation problem.* There is a serious dilemma here. A radio or television station may be sued for libel (along with the actual broadcaster) for statements made on its facilities, yet it is absolutely barred from censoring any political broadcast. In 1952 a Seattle station, however, banned a political broadcast by Senator McCarthy when he refused to delete two paragraphs which the station's attorneys considered libelous.

The Federal Communications Commission on the whole has been very severe in condemning such censorship. Its position is that the ban on political censorship in the Federal Communications Act "clearly constitutes occupation of the field by federal authority, which under law, would relieve the licensee of responsibility for libelous matter." This would be true regardless of state libel laws. There is no clear Supreme Court decision as yet on this point.

In a number of states, however, the courts do not accept

the Commission's theory and still hold stations liable. In 1955 the state of New York by statute relieved radio and television stations from libel damage resulting from defamatory statements made by legally qualified political candidates, if the station explicitly dissociated itself from the candidates' statements at the time of the broadcast.

(4) *Broadcasting of courtroom or legislative committee proceedings.* It is hardly a denial of free speech to forbid radio and television stations the right to broadcast judicial or legislative sessions. The state of New York does forbid such broadcasting, and congressional committees from time to time have also forbidden it. The only civil liberty problem which appears here is the due process right of a witness or a defendant not to be subjected to undesired nation-wide publicity. This is a very controversial question. In December, 1955, a state court in Texas allowed the televising of a trial for first-degree murder.

(5) *The "captive audience."* A minor and somewhat bizarre issue arose a few years ago on the question of whether those who ride in streetcars and buses are deprived of civil liberty when compelled against their wishes to listen to radio broadcasts while riding. The Court of Appeals in the District of Columbia held they should be protected against such broadcasting, but the Supreme Court held they were not. The broadcasts were, however, abandoned. (*Pollak* v. *Public Utilities Commission of the District of Columbia,* 191 Fed. 2d 450, 1951; reversed in 343 U.S. 451, 1952.)

(6) *Self-regulation by the industry.* Even if there is no direct official censorship of radio and television programs, there is plenty of unofficial censorship. This stems from self-interest. Like the movie industry, the radio and tele-

FREEDOM OF SPEECH AND PRESS

vision networks cannot afford to offend their millions of patrons.

The National Association of Radio and Television Broadcasters and some of the networks have set up their own codes indicating what is regarded as objectionable material and formulating what is believed to be sound broadcasting policy. These codes operate under the sanction of a "Seal of Approval" given to stations which comply. This has proved fairly effective.

The only civil liberty problem involved here is that this private censorship may go far beyond what the "public interest" requires, may tend to eliminate anything and everything which is "controversial," and may consequently prevent the fair and full use of broadcasting facilities in conformity to the principles of free speech.

The problem of blacklisting by networks will be dealt with at a later point. (*Infra*, p. 204.)

d. *Censorship in Overseas Libraries*

This of course is a problem of relatively limited importance, but in 1953–1954 it captured the public imagination and highlighted certain points. It showed how complicated and embarrassing the problems of censorship can become, how unpredictable and devastating are the political pressures which can operate in this area, and how silly we can make ourselves look in the eyes of the rest of the world without intending to do so.

The story of censorship in the overseas libraries is a rather sorry one. Congress authorized, in connection with other programs, the setting up of libraries in foreign countries occupied by United States personnel. These libraries were under the International Information Agency of the

State Department, the Mutual Security Agency, and the Point Four Program. The statute provided that these libraries were "to promote a better understanding of the United States in other countries, and to increase mutual understanding between the people of the United States and the people of other countries." Nearly two hundred such libraries were set up.

It was discovered that in these libraries were books which had been written by Communists, or by persons accused of being subversive, together with books presenting doctrines and points of view regarded as objectionable. No less than twelve directives were issued by the State Department with respect to the books in these libraries, and they represented the Department as being confused, worried, and anxious to appease critics in the matter.

By direct order of the State Department some three hundred books by forty authors were removed from these libraries, and many more were banned by United States officials overseas who felt that it would be wise to play safe. Altogether, books by nearly 250 authors were removed in various overseas libraries.

These books were banned on the following grounds: First, the books themselves were deemed to contain Communist or un-American propaganda. Second, the books had been written by Communists or other subversives, with that term defined rather broadly. Third, the books were written by authors who had pleaded the Fifth Amendment when asked about Communist affiliations. Thus in certain libraries a collection of the writings of Thomas Jefferson was removed because it had been compiled by a man who had pleaded the Fifth Amendment when quizzed by a congressional committee.

Many thoughtful persons were shocked at the idea that books should be censored by the American government on the basis of the political views of their authors rather than because of their content. President Eisenhower's comment, "Don't join the book-burners," and his statement that he did not see why Dashiell Hammett's detective stories could not safely be read, reflected widespread popular opinion but of course added to the confusion of the State Department.

The State Department finally announced that books would no longer be banned because of authorship, but there is some doubt as to whether this policy has been rigidly followed.

Certain points emerge here which have a bearing on civil liberties. First, these overseas libraries, unlike public and university libraries, are limited-purpose libraries. They cannot possibly include all books or even samples of all categories of books. The problem of deciding which books they should include is by no means simple. But, as the *Washington Post* observed, "the basis of selection should not be a blacklist, but a checklist of what the users of the library want and need." If censorship is thought necessary, it is hard to see why the broad standards applied by the United States Customs or the Post Office are not adequate. Second, it is hard to see that civil liberties in the constitutional sense are involved here. Certainly no author had a right to have his books included, and certainly no one abroad had a right to read any particular book. Third, in spite of this, the removal of books on arbitrary or unexplained grounds does create a serious injustice to the authors. The author may not have a right to have his books included, but he may properly claim that once included they should not be removed under circumstances which reflect upon his character or loyalty. Fourth, regardless of the legal situation, this policy puts the United States government in the untenable position of censoring literature on political grounds, and far worse, on grounds of the political views and behavior of authors. We appeared before the world as indulging in a flagrant repudiation of the principles of freedom of thought and expression embodied in the First Amendment.

8. Free Speech and Press in Labor Relations

The enormous growth of labor unions, their legal recognition, and the firm establishment of rights of collective bargaining have brought about some restrictions upon union activities which involve First Amendment rights.

a. *Restrictions on Labor's Political Spending*

CIO aid to the Democratic Party in the campaign of 1936 led to a demand that labor's political spending be curbed. Congress in 1943 passed the Smith-Connally Act, which forbade union contributions in connection with federal elections. The law did not extend to primaries, and there were other loopholes. It was a wartime measure and expired six months after the end of World War II.

In 1947, in the Taft-Hartley Act, Congress tightened the restrictions on political spending by labor unions by prohibiting both unions and corporations from making "expenditures" as well as "contributions" in connection with federal elections, and it required that this be applied also to primaries.

Within a week after the enactment of the Taft-Hartley Act, the CIO challenged the validity of this "expenditure" provision by publishing a political editorial written by Philip Murray in the CIO *News* endorsing a candidate for Congress in Maryland. An indictment against Philip Murray and the CIO under the "expenditure" provision of the law was dismissed on constitutional grounds by the district court. *(United States v. CIO,* 77 Fed. Supp. 355, 1948.) The Supreme Court in 1948, in *United States v. CIO* (335 U.S. 106), affirmed the dismissal, but on nonconstitutional grounds. The Court held that the Act did not intend to prohibit the kind of publicity for which Murray had been indicted. The Court expressed grave doubts about the validity of any law construed to "prohibit the publication by corporations and unions in the regular course of conducting their affairs, of periodicals advising their members, stockholders or customers of danger or advantage to their interests from the adoption of measures or the election to office of men espousing these measures."

Lower federal courts have held that labor union expenditures for newspaper and radio advertising, or for the payment to union employees of compensation for services in the campaign of a union officer for Congress, do not violate the Taft-Hartley Act. *(United States v. Painters Local Union No. 481,* 172 Fed. 2d 854, 1949; *United States v. Construction and General Laborers Union No. 264,* 101 Fed. Supp. 869, 1951.)

In July, 1955, the United Automobile Workers, CIO, was indicted for violating the "expenditure" provision of the Taft-Hartley Act by paying for political telecasts in the 1954 election in Michigan in which Senator Homer Ferguson was defeated. Perhaps the constitutionality of the provision will now be decided.

The loophole in all this legislation is found in the long-standing tradition that any organization may properly try to influence public opinion on social and economic issues if their activities are "educational" rather than political. This fine distinction has rendered the Taft-Hartley provision fairly meaningless. The CIO Political Action Committee spent in the 1952 campaign $443,258 for "educational" purposes, and the AFL spent a similarly large sum.

The efforts of the states to restrict labor's political spending have not been more successful than the efforts of Congress. Some of these state laws have been invalidated by state supreme courts as violations of freedom of speech and press, and on other grounds. *(A. F. of L. v. McAdory,* 246 Ala. 1, 1944; *A. F. of L. v. Reilly,* 113 Colo. 90, 1944; *A. F. of L. v. Mann et al.,* 188 S.W. 2d 276, 1945.) Delaware passed such a law in 1947 and repealed it in 1949. An attempt was made in Massachusetts in 1946 to prohibit political contributions by corporations or labor unions or any person acting in behalf thereof; the state supreme court held that this violated freedom of speech, press, and assembly as guaranteed by the state constitution. *(Bowe v. Secretary of Commonwealth,* 320 Mass. Repts. 230, 1946.) A similar restrictive law in Pennsylvania is still in force and has not so far been challenged. In 1955 Wisconsin passed a law prohibiting labor organizations from making political contributions.

b. *Non-Communist Affidavit—Taft-Hartley Act, 1947*

Section 9(h) of the Taft-Hartley Act resulted from widespread concern over Communist infiltration into some labor unions. It requires that every union officer file annually with the NLRB an affidavit (1) that he is not a member of the Communist Party, and (2) that he does not believe in and does not belong to any organization that "believes in or teaches the overthrow of the United States Government by force or by any illegal or unconstitutional methods." Noncomplying unions lose practically all rights under the Act. At the outset some of the major unions resisted the Act, but the resulting serious disadvantages led later to fairly widespread compliance.

In the Douds case *(American Communications Association v. Douds,* 339 U.S. 382, 1950), the Supreme Court held section 9(h) valid. Six Justices sat; five agreed that Congress could use its commerce power to deny to unions whose officers were members of the Communist Party the advantages of the Labor-Management Relations Act. The Court split evenly, however, on the question whether requiring union officers to swear that they did not believe in or belong to organizations believing in the overthrow of the government by unlawful methods infringed upon thought and belief. This judicial tie has never been broken, and thus section 9(h) was sustained.

The effect of the affidavit clause cannot be precisely judged. At first Communists in unions undertook to ignore section 9(h), but were led to comply because of the loss of privileges which resulted. By a number of devices and evasions which cannot be elaborated here, they have, however, been fairly successful in thwarting the intent of 9(h). It has proved difficult to get convictions in court for these subterfuges.

In 1952 congressional leaders were convinced that 9(h) was ineffective. Both labor and management shared this view. This conviction resulted in the wholly different approach to this problem written into the Communist Control Act of 1954, which does not require the signing of non-

Communist oaths, but which imposes drastic disabilities upon any union found, by the Attorney General after a hearing, to be "Communist-infiltrated."

c. *Picketing*

Prior to 1940, picketing was governed by the law of torts, and when injury resulted the burden rested on the picketers to show justification.

In *Thornhill* v. *Alabama,* in 1940 (310 U.S. 88), widely construed as a major victory for labor, the Supreme Court held that a state law prohibiting all picketing was an unconstitutional restriction on free speech and press and that legislative restrictions on picketing must be defended by a showing of clear and present danger (a doctrine not applied in later cases).

During and since World War II this sweeping doctrine has been substantially watered down by judicial rules creating exceptions. The present status of picketing may be summarized as follows:

(1) The free speech doctrine (Thornhill) remains, and restraints on picketing are void unless justified.

(2) No unqualified ban on peaceful picketing can be upheld unless

(a) the picketing takes place in a context of violence;

(b) there is no close economic relationship between picketers and the picketed.

(3) Picketing may be prohibited when undertaken for unlawful purposes. State and federal decisions have applied this rule where picketing was used by unions to bring about the violation of a state or federal labor law.

(4) Taft-Hartley makes picketing an unfair labor practice when used to enforce a secondary boycott (four items are spelled out in the statute).

d. *Restrictions on Free Speech of Employers*

The Wagner Act guarantees to workers the right to bargain collectively without interference or coercion by employers. This immediately imposes restrictions upon the free speech of employers, the scope and nature of which have had to be defined by the NLRB and the courts.

The NLRB at first adopted what it called the "neutrality doctrine." This assumed that the employer's power is so great that any indication of his views on labor questions would under the Act interfere with the rights of the employees. The Supreme Court lent some support to this doctrine in the statement, "Slight suggestions as to the employer's choice... may have telling effect among men who know the consequence of incurring the employer's strong displeasure." *(International Association of Machinists v. N.L.R.B.,* 311 U.S. 72, 1940.)

Strong protests by management against these rules were based upon a claim of right under the First Amendment; and subsequent decisions, both by the courts and by the NLRB, have made these limitations much less rigorous. In 1941 *(N.L.R.B. v. Virginia Electric & Power Co.,* 314 U.S. 469) the Supreme Court held that employers have a constitutional right to express their views to their workers on matters of labor policy, but at the same time it held that such expressions could be ruled to be unfair labor practices if they were either explicitly coercive or if they were coercive in the light of the employer's past conduct. This pretty well scrapped the neutrality doctrine. The Taft-Hartley Act of 1947 bolstered the free speech rights of employers substantially. It provided that employers' views or arguments are not unfair labor practices "if such expressions contain no threat of reprisal or force or promise of benefit." The NLRB, however, has tended to rule that such employer speeches are "unfair" if made in a context of coercive conduct.

The present picture with regard to employer free speech as embodied in NLRB practices is as follows:

(1) An employer's statements to his employees, if the statements contain threats of reprisal or force or promises of benefits, are unfair labor practices.

(2) Such statements, innocent on their face, may constitute unfair labor practices when considered in the context in which they are made.

(3) Noncoercive statements made by an employer to a compulsory meeting of his employees held on company property and on company time ("captive audience") are not unfair labor practices even if the union's request for an equal opportunity to reply has been denied. Such statements, however, may not be made within twenty-four hours prior to a union election.

(4) If an employer's statements to his workers have interfered with a union election, the NLRB can set the election aside, although the NLRB has shown a good deal of caution in enforcing this rule.

e. *Union Restrictions on Free Speech of Members*

On principle, a labor union should be a democratic organization. It is an agency created to represent and promote the interests of its members. At the same time, a union is an action organization, charged with the duty of furthering with maximum effectiveness the union's case in any conflict with management. In any such conflict union success is jeopardized by lack of a united union front, and this has provided an excuse, if not a valid reason, for highly centralized and even dictatorial management of many unions.

Most union constitutions have provisions which permit suppression of free political action within the union. These provisions limit the right to criticize officers or fellow members, forbid the sending out of "any letter of a scandalous or defamatory nature against any candidate for office" and, in some unions, forbid the issuing of any circular without the consent of the officers. One large union forbids any political campaigning within the union. These restrictions on the freedom of speech and press of union members can be effectively enforced through the broad disciplinary power which a union has over its members.

Whether there could or should be statutory protection for the union member's political rights inside his union need not be discussed here. What should be noted is that these rights are jeopardized probably more by his friends and protectors, the union leaders, than by his traditional enemy, management.

B. FREE SPEECH AND PRESS IN THE COURTS

1. Attitude of the Supreme Court, 1945–1950

By the end of World War II the Supreme Court had reached an all-time high in the generosity of its treatment of First Amendment rights. Two phases of the Court's free speech and press philosophy at this time warrant comment.

a. *Clear and Present Danger Doctrine*

In 1919 Justice Holmes in the Schenck case *(Schenck v. United States,* 249 U.S. 47), announced the rule of "clear and present danger" to justify punishing Schenck for distributing pamphlets urging resistance to the draft. For twenty years it was an uphill fight to get acceptance of the clear and present danger doctrine by a majority of the Court. Then, in 1937, a majority of the Court in *Herndon* v. *Lowry* (301 U.S. 242) set aside the conviction of a Communist Party organizer on the ground (among others) that his pamphlets and speeches did not constitute any clear and present danger of incitement to insurrection or offer any other threat to the public security. In 1944 the Court went further, reversing the conviction of one Hartzel on a finding of lack of clear and present danger in circumstances so similar to Schenck's that one feels certain that the 1944 Court would have set aside Schenck's conviction had it been deciding his case. *(Hartzel* v. *United States,* 322 U.S. 680, 1944.)

As we have seen, beginning with the Harry Bridges case in 1941 (p. 8) the Court had applied the clear and present danger test to contempts of court by publication. *Thornhill* v. *Alabama* (*supra,* p. 52) held a blanket antipicketing statute void on its face for lack of showing of clear and present danger to justify its enactment—a rather revolutionary extension of the rule which up to then had been applied as a "rule of reason" in the application of statutes rather than as a measure of the validity of the statute itself.

b. *"Preferred Status" of First Amendment Rights*

In the second place, a group of Justices in the forties announced the doctrine that First Amendment rights occupy a "preferred place" in our scale of constitutional values, so that a law which on its face abridges those rights no longer enjoys the traditional presumption of constitutionality. Whether designed to do so or not, this doctrine had the effect of taking liberal judges off the hook in cases where adherents to the Holmesian doctrine (of utmost judicial tolerance for legislation) were forced to presume the validity of laws whittling down First Amendment rights. By the "preferred status" doctrine, most clearly set out by Justice Rutledge in *Thomas* v. *Collins* (323 U.S. 516, 1945), laws impinging on First Amendment rights do not enjoy the usual presumption of constitutionality, and the burden of proving them valid can be met only by a showing of clear and present danger.

There was of course nothing new in the idea that some parts of the Bill of Rights are more important than others. This distinction was embodied in the early 1900s in the Insular cases, in which the Court had to determine how much of the Bill of Rights "follows the flag" into "unincorporated" American territories. *(Hawaii* v. *Mankichi,* 190 U.S. 197, 1903.) The Court has drawn a similar line in deciding which parts of the Bill of Rights are assimilated into the due process clause of the Fourteenth Amendment and are thus made applicable to the states. *(Palko* v. *Connecticut,* 302 U.S. 319, 1937.)

This doctrine of the "preferred status" of First Amendment rights probably never commanded the support of the full majority of the Court. It is widely hailed, however, by civil libertarians off the Court.

2. Changes in the Supreme Court's Attitude since 1950

Since the deaths of Justices Murphy and Rutledge in 1949, changes have been apparent in the Court's decisions on First Amendment rights. These are explained partly by shifting judicial personnel and partly perhaps by the changing character of free speech problems. These changes are as follows:

a. *Clear and Present Danger*

The clear and present danger doctrine has not been abandoned in ordinary free speech cases, but the Court seems uncertain and fluctuating in its findings of clear and present danger. This appears in the Court's difficulty in dealing with the problem of sound trucks. It is more obvious when one compares the Court's decision in the Terminiello case (*Terminiello* v. *City of Chicago,* 337 U.S. 1, 1949)—in which the Court found invalid a city ordinance which made it disorderly conduct to indulge in a highly inflammatory antiracial speech which actually resulted in disorder—with the Feiner case *(Feiner* v. *New York,* 340 U.S. 315, 1951)—which upheld the conviction for disorderly conduct of a student soapbox orator addressing seventy-five people in a side street in Syracuse. The presumptions in support of free speech and press seem rather less firm than formerly.

b. *"Preferred Status"*

The "preferred status" of First Amendment rights seems to have passed into the discard. Justice Frankfurter never accepted the doctrine, and he has said so bluntly. It is still sometimes mentioned in dissents by Justices Douglas and Black.

c. *Criminal Conspiracy*

In cases under the Smith Act where the Court has dealt with what it regards as "criminal conspiracy," the traditional test of clear and present danger has been drastically modified, if not in fact abandoned. Of five opinions in the

Dennis case *(Dennis v. United States,* 341 U.S. 494, 1951), four dealt with clear and present danger. Justices Douglas and Black dissented on the ground that no clear and present danger existed. Justice Jackson, concurring, bluntly declared that the clear and present danger test has no applicability to a criminal conspiracy and was never intended to have and that it should be kept for cases involving ordinary kinds of restrictions on speech and press. Justice Vinson, writing for four members of the Court, adopted Judge Learned Hand's rewriting of the rule to make it read "clear and probable danger." Justice Frankfurter, who has never been fond of the clear and present danger rule, felt that the issues in the Dennis case were those of conflict of interest which the Court itself must decide; this is very close to assimilating the rule to due process of law. It may be noted that Justices Hughes and Stone had never alluded to clear and present danger, but had decided Fourteenth Amendment free speech and press cases on a simple due process basis.

Certainly the Court in the Dennis case read the time element out of clear and present danger, and the time element was perhaps its most unique aspect. It is too early to say whether, by recent decisions, free speech and press have lost a portion of their earlier protection.

d. *Censorship*

In censorship cases the Supreme Court has broadened judicial protection to the press and to motion pictures. This, however, has rested in the main on the Court's insistence that criminal laws relating to publications or films must meet the long-established due process test of reasonable certainty. The law must be clear enough to permit a reasonable man to know when he is violating it. Recent efforts to censor have failed to meet this test in several important cases. As we have seen elsewhere (p. 11), however, this does not mean that obscenity is protected by the First Amendment.

C. FREEDOM OF ASSEMBLY

Historically, the right of assembly was the right to assemble in order to petition. It has long since become an independent right similar in status to that of speech and press.

By the end of World War II freedom of assembly enjoyed substantial judicial protection. In 1937 in the DeJonge case *(DeJonge* v. *Oregon,* 299 U.S. 353) the Supreme Court held that DeJonge, a Communist, could lawfully address a meeting called by the Communist Party in order to discuss a strike. In 1939 the Court held in *Hague* v. *CIO* (307 U.S. 496) that Jersey City could not give to its Director of Public Safety power to refuse permits for public meetings on the streets, parks, or public buildings on the ground that such refusal was for the purpose of preventing riots, disturbances, or disorderly assemblages. (It was pretty clear that Mayor Hague's henchmen would provide the necessary disorder if the meetings were held.) In 1945 *Thomas* v. *Collins* (323 U.S. 516) held that freedom of assembly is abridged by requiring a union official to register with public authorities before soliciting union membership.

There are relatively few cases dealing squarely with freedom of assembly. It tends quite naturally to get merged with freedom of speech.

Current issues regarding freedom of assembly are as follows:

(1) The police power naturally and properly restricts freedom of assembly. The community can properly guard against riot and disorder and may also enforce safety and traffic regulations. However, broad authority to prevent public meetings because of the fear of disorder is a dangerously restrictive power. It may well bring about, as it did in Jersey City, a complete ban on all public meetings, since the fear of disorder can always be conjured up.

(2) The kind and scope of administrative discretion given to public officers who issue permits and licenses to hold public meetings present crucial civil liberty problems. If the discretion is too broad, the right of assembly may cease to exist.

(3) Freedom of assembly may be limited by the proprietary interest which a town or city has in its public buildings, schoolhouses, and the like.

(a) The complete refusal of authorities to allow any public meetings in school buildings can properly be defended as long as no exceptions are made which would spell discrimination.

(b) If meetings are allowed, the question arises as to what kind of meetings may be barred. Can any claim be made to the right of equality of treatment in enjoying the privilege of using the buildings? There is a current tendency to forbid the use of public buildings by groups loosely described as "Fascist, Communist, or subversive." In 1946, however, the Supreme Court of California held invalid a statute prohibiting the use of public school buildings by "subversive" groups, when such use was permitted for civic purposes generally. *(Danskin v. San Diego Unified School District,* 28 Cal. 2d 536, 1946.)

The use of public buildings is currently being denied by public authorities to groups regarded as "controversial." In 1954 the Board of Education in Yonkers refused to allow the Yonkers Committee for Peace to meet in a school building. This action was taken on the ground that the State Board of Education had instructed school boards to bar "controversial" meetings. This raises the question whether the First Amendment was not intended to protect the kind of speeches and meetings which are "controversial." In *Ellis* v. *Dixon* (349 U.S. 458, 1955) the Supreme Court refused to decide the case on its merits because of the insufficiency of the petitioner's pleadings.

(4) The doctrine that the Communist Party is a criminal conspiracy, a doctrine supported in the Dennis case *(supra,* p. 58), would provide a basis for refusing to allow almost any official meeting held by the Party. It will be noted that this doctrine that the Party is a criminal conspiracy had not been developed when the DeJonge case was decided in 1937.

(5) Important restrictions, not of a strictly legal variety, are placed upon freedom of assembly as a result of the inference as to loyalty and security drawn from a man's attendance at meetings also attended by Communists or subversives. Such attendance, if known, will almost certainly become "derogatory" information in the case of an employee of the government, and it is very likely to lead to his dismissal. The operation here of the doctrine of guilt by association seriously restricts the citizen's exercise of his freedom of assembly.

(6) We have seen in the labor cases (p. 52) that picketing

is a form of free speech and press. Is it also a form of free assembly? A number of bills forbidding picketing the White House have been introduced into Congress since the Rosenberg case, when such picketing was very persistent. The Subversive Activities Control Act of 1950 forbids the picketing of any United States court for the purpose of obstructing justice. Disorder resulting from the picketing can, of course, be dealt with. Political picketing as a rule would seem to be less vulnerable than picketing during a strike, since political picketing normally has no element of intimidation of bystanders or any purpose of boycotting anyone. There are no cases on this point.

(7) There is little or no protection against private interference with freedom of assembly unless that protection is accorded by the police. No constitutional right of the citizen is invaded by such private interference. Three Supreme Court Justices in the Hague case (p. 60) argued that the right to assemble to discuss rights under the Wagner Act is a privilege of United States citizenship and is therefore protected by the Civil Rights Act. It is doubtful whether this could be called a doctrine of the Court, and its application is very limited at best. There is no legal relief against the activities of private pressure groups which persuade public authorities to deny the use of public buildings to unpopular minority groups.

D. FREEDOM OF PETITION

The First Amendment establishes the right "to petition the Government for redress of grievances." This limited language has long been interpreted broadly to create a right of petition including "demands for the exercise by the Government of its powers in furtherance of the interests and prosperity of the petitioners, and of their views on politically contentious matters." Anyone who reads the *Congressional Record* is aware that the right of petition is exercised daily. Any member of Congress can file petitions with the Clerk, and as a matter of routine they are printed in the *Congressional Record* unless in the judgment of the Speaker they are obscene or insulting.

It is obvious that a petition, like any other piece of writing, is subject to the traditional restraints relating to obscenity, libel, incitement to crime, and so on. In World War I, twenty-seven South Dakota farmers circulated a petition in opposition to the draft and other war policies. They were sentenced to prison for more than a year, but on appeal the government confessed error and the conviction was reversed. (*United States* v. *Baltzer et al.*, 248 U.S. 593, 1918.)

1. Petitions Not Contempts of Court

Attempts have been made by some judges from time to time to regard petitions as contempts of court. This view has not prevailed in the appellate courts. The Supreme Court held in the Harry Bridges case (*supra*, p. 8) that the contempt citation of Bridges for sending his telegram to the Secretary of Labor amounted to an abridgment of his right of petition. In 1953 the Supreme Court of Illinois overruled a contempt citation by a circuit judge against members of the Good Government Council who had petitioned the judge to appoint a special prosecutor to proceed with indictments for embezzlement against a justice of the peace. *(People* v. *Howarth,* 415 Ill. 501, 1953.) There seems to be ample judicial protection against this sort of thing.

2. Lobbying

A currently unanswered question is whether legislation which regulates lobbying is an invalid restriction of the right of petition. It is generally agreed that lobbying is an exercise of that right. It has grown to enormous and disturbing proportions. In 1946 Congress passed the Federal Regulation of Lobbying Act which requires the registration with the government of all lobbyists and the filing of statements by their principals of amounts of money spent. The lower courts have cast grave doubts upon the validity of this statute. *(National Association of Manufacturers* v. *McGrath,* 103 Fed. Supp. 510, 1952.) It seems clear that Congress may properly punish dishonest or corrupt forms of lobbying. Whether in this statute it has invaded the right of petition remains an open question.

In the Rumely case in 1953 *(United States* v. *Rumely,* 345 U.S. 41) the Supreme Court defined lobbying as "persuasion exerted upon members of Congress," and it implied that Congress could not validly limit the efforts of lobbyists to influence public opinion.

3. Guilt by Association

Discouragement of the exercise of the right of petition, informal but nonetheless effective, is one of the end results of the doctrine of guilt by association. Stigma attaches to one who signs a petition (many did petition the President in 1933 to recognize Russia) which has also been signed by Communists or fellow travelers. Names on petitions will be carefully checked by officers administering loyalty and security programs.

E. PRIVATE CURBS ON SPEECH AND PRESS

The First and Fourteenth Amendments give protection only against invasions of freedom of speech and press by government, not by individuals. It is obvious, however, that one's right to speak or to publish may be interfered with by his neighbors or by various private groups in the community. Unless the private obstruction of these rights takes the form of disorderly conduct or of some other breach of the peace, or of a tort, there is no legal redress.

It is obvious, however, that in the broader view these important civil liberties are impaired by private interference. Elsewhere the problems of the private censorship of textbooks and the important problem of private blacklisting are dealt with. (*Infra,* p. 203.)

Private restrictions on First Amendment rights take various forms. We have already discussed (p. 44) the self-censorship which prevails in radio and television. Clearly the only rights of speech or press which are impaired here are the rights of the community to read, see, and listen interpreted on the broadest possible basis. No rights of the industry itself are impaired since the limitations are self-imposed.

In the second place, various minority groups undertake to impose their taboos on the rest of the community in the matter of literature, motion pictures, and radio and television programs.

The problem of obscenity, as has been suggested before, arouses the crusading instincts of many private organizations who desire more rigid restrictions than the law imposes. The Catholic Church, through its Legion of Decency, has long been in the vanguard of this movement.

It is supported by a considerable number of other organizations devoted to encouraging "clean literature," and so on.

The censorship activities of various patriotic groups such as the American Legion and the DAR are well known. These groups indicate their disapproval of various types of literature, public speeches, meetings, movies, and radio and television programs, and they undertake to bring about compliance with their wishes in these matters.

A third type of private censorship has arisen within the past few decades. This is the campaign of various racial groups to bring about the elimination from literature and art of everything which places members of the race in a humiliating or undignified position in the public mind or eye. Thus, *Uncle Tom's Cabin*, *The Merchant of Venice*, and works by Stephen Foster and Gilbert and Sullivan have all been edited in an effort to get rid of such allusions to Negroes or Jews as are thought to be derogatory or uncomplimentary. Recently the NAACP has turned its guns on Amos and Andy as well as Beulah and Rochester.

The civil liberty issue involved in these forms of censorship does not lie in the efforts of minority groups to express their disapproval of, or withdraw their support from, literature, plays, and other materials which offend them. The issue does arise, however, when these minority groups undertake to impose economic boycotts against publishers, theater owners, or others who refuse to enforce this private censorship. The principle may be stated in this way: Any minority group has the right to propagandize its own views with regard to objectionable literature or art. It is well within its rights in doing so. The general public, on the other hand, should be protected in its freedom to see, read, and hear everything save that which is in conflict with established law. The issue is pointed up by saying that a person's right to boycott a movie which he thinks is objectionable should not extend to a secondary boycott by which he undertakes to run the movie or theater out of business for showing the picture he does not like.

SELECTED READINGS

Reading on the problems of freedom of thought and expression might well begin with John Stuart Mill's classic *Essay on Liberty* (1859), available in a number of editions. Of great value is Zechariah Chafee's *Free Speech in the United States* (Cambridge: Harvard University Press, 1941). Also by Chafee is the booklet, *Freedom of Speech and Press* (New York: Carrie Chapman Catt Memorial Fund, Inc., 1955). Alexander Meiklejohn, *Free Speech in Its Relation to Self-Government* (New York: Harper, 1948), contends that freedom of political discussion should be regarded as an absolute right; while Thomas I. Cook, *Democratic Rights versus Communist Activity* (New York: Doubleday, 1954), defends restrictions upon some types of political discussion and propaganda. A useful selection of Supreme Court cases on freedom of speech and press is found in Milton R. Konvitz, *Bill of Rights Reader* (Ithaca: Cornell University Press, 1954). Howard Mumford Jones (editor), *Primer of Intellectual Freedom* (Cambridge: Harvard University Press, 1949), is a valuable small collection of notable statements on freedom of thought and expression from Milton, Jefferson, and Mill down to the present time.

The Commission on the Freedom of the Press (financed by Time, Inc.) published in 1947 through the Chicago University Press a series of valuable monographs. Of these the most notable was Zechariah Chafee, *Government and Mass Communications,* in two volumes. Others were: William E. Hocking, *Freedom of the Press;* Llewellyn White, *The American Radio;*

FREEDOM OF SPEECH AND PRESS

and Ruth A. Inglis, *Freedom of the Movies*. William L. Chenery, *Freedom of the Press* (New York: Harcourt, Brace, 1955), gives a veteran editor's appraisal of the "never-ending fight against arbitrary censorship" in its various forms. Censorship is also dealt with in Paul Blanshard, *The Right to Read—The Battle against Censorship* (Boston: Beacon Press, 1955), and in Anne Lyon Haight, *Banned Books* (New York: R. R. Bowker Co., 1955). An older book on the subject is Morris Ernst and Alexander Lindey, *The Censor Marches On: Recent Milestones in the Administration of Obscenity Law in the United States* (New York: Doubleday, 1940). *Newsletter on Intellectual Freedom* (Yellow Springs: Intellectual Freedom Committee, American Library Association, irregularly four times a year), records current happenings in the field of censorship and intellectual freedom.

Philip Wittenberg, *Dangerous Words: A Guide to the Law of Libel* (New York: Columbia University Press, 1947), presents a complex and technical subject in a manner intelligible to the layman.

Freedom of assembly is dealt with in Bradford Smith, *A Dangerous Freedom* (Philadelphia: Lippincott, 1954).

· II ·

Academic Freedom

ACADEMIC freedom is an elusive subject to deal with. It has fewer sharp edges than most problems which are equally important. The conflicts of interest and sincere differences of opinion with regard to it are numerous and persistent.

Academic freedom is not a civil liberty in the orthodox sense. It is a First Amendment right only when the teacher's freedom of speech and press—the same rights which are enjoyed by all citizens—happen to be involved. Academic freedom is not a legally enforceable right except when certain fringe matters, such as contracts of employment, are involved. What we speak of as academic freedom is the result of a tradition of long standing, and it is based on the concept that "a university is a center of independent thought without which the process of research and higher education cannot go on." Restrictions on that independent thought would defeat the purpose of the whole enterprise. We think of academic freedom most commonly as applied to colleges and universities; but it is just as true that on the public school level sound education cannot be carried on in an atmosphere of intellectual restraint in which there is constant insistence upon conformity.

Since the present analysis does not confine itself simply to the problems of higher education but includes education on any level, certain distinctions should be made which will indicate why clear-cut summaries of academic freedom problems are difficult to make.

A. DISTINCTIONS BETWEEN EDUCATIONAL INSTITUTIONS

1. Denominational Schools

Not all schools and colleges pretend to grant academic freedom as commonly defined. Denominational and sectarian institutions are the clearest examples. In these institutions religious orthodoxy is required, and presumably a man invited to teach in one of them is aware of these limitations when he enters his employment and can hardly plead a breach of academic freedom if he is required to adhere to the doctrines for which the school stands.

This is similarly true of any other institution which advertises itself as advocating or teaching a particular doctrine or point of view. The southern millionaire who tried a few years ago to give money to a college if it would teach the doctrine of white supremacy found it impossible to do so; but had he succeeded, one could hardly say that there would be a breach of academic freedom in requiring teachers in such a college to teach the specified doctrines. One who did not wish to do so would have had ample advance warning of the requirements.

2. Tax-supported Colleges and Universities

Tax-supported colleges and universities have academic freedom problems differing somewhat from those of privately endowed institutions. Theoretically the standards of academic freedom in all colleges and universities, whether tax-supported or endowed, should be the same; in some cases they are. Viewed realistically, however, tax-supported institutions are in certain respects uniquely vulnerable to the undermining of academic freedom.

In the first place, they are often more directly subject to political pressures. The state legislature must pass upon the university budget. A professor of agricultural economics in a farm state who openly opposes agricultural price support may find himself in trouble with the rural lawmakers, and the institution in which he teaches may also find itself in trouble. In addition, there are indirect pressures on state universities which stem from the idea that they are publicly owned and supported, that the right to attend them is the common right of all young citizens of the state, and that there should therefore be a considerable amount of supervision over what goes on in them. This idea undoubtedly lay back of the Texas statute of 1952 barring from state-supported colleges and universities all students who do not take an oath that for the two years previous they had not belonged to an organization advocating the violent overthrow of government.

Private institutions also are vulnerable to equal, though perhaps differing, outside pressures resulting from their need to secure private financial support. Moreover, immunity from political pressure enjoyed by private institutions may disappear with the growing of the idea that tax exemptions may be withdrawn from institutions that do not conform to various standards set by governmental authorities.

3. Tax-supported Public Schools

Well-recognized differences exist between the colleges and universities and the public school systems of the country. The extent and nature of academic freedom will vary sharply here, first because students who are immature cannot be subjected to quite the same teaching, including possible indoctrination, to which college and university students can be subjected; and second, because public schools are in a most direct sense not only community property but institutions in which the community itself has the keenest and most direct interest, so that the degree of community supervision and control over them is bound to be very great.

B. BASIC CODE OF ACADEMIC FREEDOM— WIDELY ACCEPTED PRINCIPLES

With these distinctions in mind, one may summarize generally the accepted principles of academic freedom. There will of course be controversy over individual points, but in general there is a rough consensus.

1. Freedom of Speech, Writing, and Research

The freedom of the teacher to speak, write, and carry on research is the most basic aspect of academic freedom. He is, of course, subject to all of the recognized limitations upon First Amendment rights such as those relating to obscenity, libel, incitement to crime, and so on, but beyond that he enjoys complete freedom save as it is limited by the self-imposed standards of his profession. He is free to deal with controversial matters, to state his own opinions, and to carry on investigations in the field of his own choice. Naturally the farther down one goes in the educational system the greater are the normal restrictions upon the teacher resulting from a rigid curriculum and the need to conform to an established school program.

The freedom here discussed includes freedom from censorship and from the reporting of the contents of the teacher's classroom lectures. Back in 1917 President Lowell at Harvard emphasized the importance of keeping the teacher free from this kind of snooping, and in the current Sweezy case in New Hampshire the crucial issue has been the refusal of Dr. Sweezy to disclose publicly the contents of classroom lectures. (*New Hampshire, by Wyman, Attorney General,* v. *Sweezy,* pending in the state supreme court.)

2. Freedom of Public Discussion in the Academic Community

An accepted principle of academic freedom is that the teacher should be entitled to speak freely outside the classroom on matters which claim his interest.

Particularly in colleges and universities academic freedom is considered impaired if outside speakers and scholars may not freely be invited to the campus by the university or by faculty groups for the public discussion of any lawful topics. This problem was sharply highlighted by an order of the trustees of Ohio State University in 1951 which forbade outside lecturers to appear on the campus without the approval of the president of the university. The order was issued after the appearance on the campus of speakers who expressed controversial social and economic views. This ban was so sharply criticized in the bitter controversy which ensued that finally the trustees retreated and the ban was lifted.

3. Textbooks, Teaching Materials, and Curriculum

It is an accepted rule that in colleges and universities decisions with regard to all of these matters belong in the hands of the individual professor, the department, or the faculty.

On the public school level, however, teachers cannot be permitted this degree of individual choice, since there must be some uniformity in textbooks and teaching materials in order to permit the meeting of common standards. Yet surely the decisions on these important matters should be made by educators who have professional training, and not by politicians or laymen. The attempts of amateurs to control these matters have been uniformly unfortunate. On the twenty-fifth anniversary of the Scopes trial an effort is being made to get the Tennessee legislature to repeal the notorious antievolution statute which is still in force.

Practically every state in the Union requires by law the teaching in the public schools of American history, or the Constitution, or various matters described as "patriotism." These are positive requirements rather than restraints. There can be no objection to them except as they require some special indoctrination.

4. The Teacher as a Citizen—Political Activity and Associations

The teacher's right to organize into unions is now pretty widely recognized, but only after a hard-fought battle. He also enjoys the right to be a member of any political party, although it will be remembered that some men were dismissed from teaching positions for voting for William Jennings Bryan back in 1896. The right to join any lawful organization and to take part in its activities is recognized. To an increasing degree the right of the teacher to run for political office, assuming that this is compatible with his academic duties, is recognized.

In the enjoyment of all of these rights of citizenship the teaching profession has been quick to recognize a corresponding responsibility. The professor or teacher is bound to be associated in the public mind with his own institution, and he bears a responsibility to represent it fairly and not discreditably. He is under an obligation to be accurate, to show respect for the opinions of others, and to dissociate himself and his opinions from his own school or college.

5. Tenure of Teachers

While the protection of tenure is perhaps not a substantive right in itself, it is certainly necessary to the sense of security on which academic freedom is based. It distinguishes the teacher from the employee who may be dismissed for no other reason that that his employer wishes to dispense with his services. The problems of tenure are so important that they merit the most thorough study and appraisal.

a. *Probationary Tenure*

Tenure does not mean permanent tenure for every teacher. The probationary status given to assistant professors, instructors, and younger teachers generally through the device of term appointments does not impair academic freedom. This arrangement is necessary in order to determine professional fitness with a view to promotion.

Problems arise, however, when the failure to reappoint

instructors or assistant professors for causes not relating to their competence amounts to actual dismissal for causes which spell out invasions of academic freedom.

b. *Valid Reasons for Dismissal*

It has always been recognized that teachers or professors may be dismissed for incompetence, dishonesty, physical or mental incapacity, conviction of a felony involving moral turpitude, and similar carefully defined misconduct. There are, of course, always borderline cases.

There is no such thing as permanent tenure. The right to dismiss a professor or teacher for cause always exists. Whether such dismissals invade academic freedom depends upon what these causes are.

c. *Procedures for Dismissal or Discipline—"Due Process"*

Proper procedures for dismissal include an adequate hearing before the action is taken. In colleges and universities, judgment of a man's colleagues should be sought because of their special knowledge of the problems involved, though their judgment usually cannot legally be made the final one. Sensible rules of evidence should prevail in these hearings. This means the rejection of pure hearsay evidence as well as the barring of secret evidence. The man involved is entitled to confront those who have accused him.

6. Freedom for Students

Certain organizations have, in the past decade, come to regard freedom for students as a part of academic freedom. The American Civil Liberties Union has drafted an elaborate code embodying the freedoms which it is thought students ought to enjoy.

a. *Freedom of Expression on the Campus*

It is accepted without question that a student should be entitled to express freely his political, economic, social, and religious views, that student publications should be free from prior censorship, and that although student editors may be disciplined for misconduct they should not be punished for the printing of unpopular views.

There is sharp conflict with regard to the extent of the right of student groups to bring outside speakers to the campus. Many colleges and universities exercise rigid control over the selection of such speakers. There is, however, growing support for the plan to have the student organizations thoroughly scrutinized at the time they are authorized by the faculty and then to allow them complete freedom in the matter of inviting outside speakers. The university thus dissociates itself completely from these speakers. This policy is followed at Columbia, Harvard, and Wisconsin. A model plan embodying this scheme has the support of the American Council of Education.

b. *Freedom off the Campus*

It is generally agreed that off the campus a student should enjoy the same rights any other citizen enjoys with regard to his activities. A legitimate restriction here is that students should not represent themselves as speaking or acting for the school, college, or university, and their use of the school name may properly be limited.

c. *Freedom to "Join"*

The student's freedom to form or join organizations has been a controversial question. It has been generally felt, however, that this right should not be restrained as long as legal boundaries are not overstepped.

d. *Freedom of Conscience*

It is generally held that, except in denominational schools, students should be free from compulsion, restraint, or discrimination because of their religious beliefs. In this connection colleges and universities should make appropriate recognition of the position of conscientious objectors, since it has long been accepted national policy to do so.

e. *Fair Procedures in Matters of Discipline*

There can be no doubt, of course, of the right of school authorities to exercise proper discipline over students. In colleges and universities it has come to be agreed that serious discipline should be imposed only after a fair hearing in which the student is permitted to defend himself, with the assistance of some adult friend or member of the faculty, and that there should be fair and clear standards of conduct and misconduct by which the student is guided.

f. *Student Training in the Democratic Process*

Here would be included the right of students to petition the faculty on matters in which students have a direct concern. This would include curriculum and similar topics. Student self-government in colleges and universities is on the increase. The operation, by student officers chosen by the students themselves, of honor systems and other disciplinary codes has come to be regarded as important and desirable. There is a tendency to increase student participation in matters of student conduct and student affairs by allowing the students to act in a consultative role to faculty committees and to administrative officers in such cases. Student morale is thus improved and wiser decisions are made.

C. CURRENT PROBLEMS OF ACADEMIC FREEDOM

It is inevitable that the current drive against communism and disloyalty should have an impact upon academic freedom. It is widely urged that the methods employed to discover whether and to what extent our schools and colleges are "infiltrated" with subversives, or our students are being dangerously "indoctrinated," can hardly fail to leave their impress upon the free intellectual life of the school or university. A number of problems have arisen in this area.

1. Loyalty Oaths for Teachers

The problem of the loyalty oath is being intensively studied. Oath requirements are by no means new. For many years teachers in tax-supported schools in more than twenty states have been required to take oaths to support the constitutions of the United States and of the state. These have had little practical impact, save to annoy a certain number of teachers who resent the idea that teachers need to be singled out for this sort of thing.

Test oaths designed to disclose past loyalty or disloyalty are a very different matter. These are being increasingly employed as part of the routine for testing fitness for employment in public schools and state-supported universities. These oaths vary in form, ranging from a simple sworn statement that one is not a member of the Communist Party and has not been such for a fixed period of years, to an oath that one is not and has not been a member of any organization described as subversive by the Attorney General, by various legislative committees, or by other authorities.

The refusal to take these oaths usually results in dismissal. It has been established that some of the people who have refused to take them have done so because of their resentment against the imposition of the oath rather than because of any disloyalty in their past.

If one knowingly takes the oath falsely, he is guilty of perjury. Thus far no case is recalled of a teacher's being prosecuted for this kind of false swearing.

2. Dismissals on Loyalty Grounds

a. *Communist Party Membership*

It is widely accepted that membership in the Communist Party is a ground for dismissing a teacher or professor. The problem is of course uncomplicated in the few states in which membership in the Communist Party is unlawful. There are, however, sharp differences of opinion with regard to the broader issue, and these differences turn on the question whether an avowed Communist can be regarded as competent to share in the intellectual life of a school or college. It is urged that university teaching must be fairminded and objective and that present membership in the Communist Party creates a very powerful presumption of incompetence to teach, a presumption reasonably arising from the loss of intellectual independence incurred by those who are obligated to follow the Communist Party line. Ardent liberals divide sharply on the question as to whether Communist Party membership does of necessity imply loss of intellectual freedom, but our schools and colleges are operating on the principle that it does.

b. *Other Grounds for Questioning Loyalty*

Other much less clear evidences of disloyalty form the basis for dismissals. The range is very wide. In New York

State the Feinberg Act (which requires no loyalty oath) calls for the dismissal of teachers in tax-supported schools and colleges who are members of organizations found by the Regents, after proper procedures, to be subversive. The New York City Board of Education last June issued a rule that teachers who are or have been members of the Communist Party may be required to inform on their fellow teachers with respect to possible Communist affiliations and may be dismissed if they refuse to inform. Bitter controversy is still raging over this requirement. The State Teachers College in Kansas relieved a professor of his duties because he signed a petition for the pardon of the eleven Communist leaders. The Pennsylvania Board of Education dismissed twenty-six teachers (questioned by the Velde Committee) on technical charges of incompetence; one of these was told that she had shown poor judgment by "being in a position to be called before the Committee." It cannot be stated that such examples are typical. Furthermore, the number of teachers dismissed on loyalty grounds is very small.

c. *Procedures for Dismissals*

In some places procedures for the dismissal of professors and secondary school teachers have come to be somewhat more arbitrary under the pressure of these loyalty requirements. Fair and open hearings are supposed to be the rule; but hearsay evidence, secret testimony, and other deviations from the rules of procedural fair play have sometimes prevailed. There are cases in which there have been no procedures at all, just dismissal.

Here may be mentioned the development of systems of espionage on campuses and in the school systems. A national student organization with chapters in many colleges and universities sprang up to carry on such espionage through student agents who report to the local FBI what they observe. Senator Jenner reports that in California there are some twenty colleges in which "contact" men have been planted to observe and report subversive activities to congressional investigating committees. These men are regular security officers, frequently former FBI agents. Testimony before the Jenner Committee stated that the findings in these colleges are made available to other institutions, and that some one hundred teachers have been dismissed and another hundred barred from appointment on the basis of information secured in this way. These statements are not documented.

3. Congressional Investigations of Schools and Colleges

It is admitted that congressional committees have no power over schools and colleges. They cannot dismiss any teacher or professor. They can only expose and harass. The central issue here is this: Assuming that the investigation of the loyalty of teachers is thought necessary, are these committees fit for the task? They have no wide knowledge of college or university problems, and too often they apply standards and tests irrelevant to the question of professional fitness. The educational world generally inclines to the view that outsiders should not undertake this job.

The impact of these investigations upon academic freedom has been extremely sharp. Evidence is accumulating, based on competent investigations, that this steady drive in the direction of conformity has resulted in the intimidation of teachers and has created in them a zeal to stay away from "controversial matters."

Refusal to co-operate with congressional committees in giving testimony is an accepted basis for dismissal, although in some cases the refusal rests upon the teacher's resentment against the intrusion of the committee into fields where he feels it does not belong, and not upon any fear that he might incriminate himself. College and university administrators have generally urged faculty members to extend full co-operation to investigating committees.

4. Teachers and Professors Who Invoke the Fifth Amendment

Some professors and teachers summoned before investigating bodies have pleaded the protection against self-incrimination in the Fifth Amendment and have refused to answer questions. Almost every teacher who has pleaded the Fifth Amendment and has persisted in doing so has lost his job. There is sharp controversy here. Is the pleading of the Fifth Amendment evidence of unfitness to be a teacher? This is not a simple question. Does such pleading indicate a concealment of actual guilt, a basic lack of candor, or merely a conscientious stubbornness which implies no moral turpitude? The problem has not been made easier by the fact that teachers are still out in front in point of numbers of those who have pleaded the Fifth Amendment for legally untenable reasons. Some have done so for the alleged purpose of obstructing the inquiry, others for the alleged purpose of avoiding the giving of evidence against their friends. Neither position is tenable in terms of constitutional law.

The teacher who refuses, without pleading the Fifth

Amendment, and without challenging the constitutional authority of the committee, to answer questions about his associates on "grounds of honor and conscience" is, of course, actually taking the position of a conscientious objector.

For a more general discussion of the Fifth Amendment, see *infra,* p. 140.

5. Controls on Loyalty Grounds of Other Interests in the Academic Community

a. *Screening of Outside Speakers*

The bitter controversy at Ohio State University created by the ban on speakers set up by the Board of Trustees in 1951 has been alluded to. By this device the trustees, acting through the president, undertook to bar from the university campus any speakers of whom they disapproved. They were required by the pressure of opinion to retreat from this position. In 1955 the president of the University of Washington refused to allow Robert Oppenheimer to address a conference of scientists on the campus. It appears that in some institutions persons who have been associated with organizations listed as possibly subversive, or persons who have pleaded the Fifth Amendment, would not be permitted to speak.

b. *Textbooks, Teaching Materials, and Libraries*

There is always some agitation to "cleanse" schools of textbooks which are not considered safe. This "cleansing" would apply, of course, to any Communist propaganda. Books in economics and sociology have been barred because they do not pay proper respect to the "American system of free enterprise."

In some places, and notably in some cities in California, the publications of UNESCO have been specifically barred from the schools. Where isolationist sentiments are strong, textbook writers are being put under pressure to delete favorable comments about the United Nations and other forms of international co-operation.

An extension of this movement is the drive to ban books written by authors who are suspect on loyalty grounds. In 1952 a Texas statute forbade the State Board of Education to adopt or buy any book for schools unless the author (if living, and otherwise the publisher) had filed a three-point, all-inclusive loyalty oath.

In New York state the Board of Regents in 1951 set up a subcommittee to review complaints made against textbooks used in the New York schools. After a period of two years no complaints had been received and no action of any kind was taken.

In 1951 the Indiana Superintendent of Public Instruction announced that he had invited nineteen Catholic priests to assist him in the screening of school textbooks "for traces of Communism or subversive influence."

c. *Student Organizations*

The problems involved here have already been discussed (p. 77), but it is pertinent to point out here that students can be pushed around more arbitrarily than teachers, and there is a current disposition here and there to impose restrictions upon them.

6. SECRECY—CLASSIFIED RESEARCH ON THE CAMPUS

An important problem in academic freedom stems from the participation of many of our large universities in the research programs of the government. There is every reason why universities should serve the government freely, and most of them do. The problem arises when government research contracts are entered into which require absolute secrecy from, as well as the highest possible security clearance for, not only the scientist engaged in the research but for everyone in any way in contact with the enterprise. Many large universities have refused these "classified contracts." Chemists and physicists point out that to become involved in such an enterprise cuts them completely off from the normal activities of the teacher, since they are forbidden to give students any of the information or experience connected with the government enterprise. In 1953 fourteen universities refused to enter into contracts with the Defense Department to offer correspondence courses to men and women in the armed services because government regulations would have authorized the Department to "disapprove" faculty members conducting the courses. There can be no doubt that the carrying on of classified research in a university has a serious impact on academic freedom.

7. Dangers to Academic Freedom from Those Who Finance Education

a. *Tax Appropriations*

As it has already been noted (p. 71), serious problems of academic freedom arise from the fact that political bodies, both state and local, levy the taxes and appropriate the funds by which tax-supported schools and colleges are run. It is to be hoped that the political pressures so obviously lurking in the background and so obviously in a position to impair academic freedom can be kept under restraint.

b. *Federal Aid*

Some distinguished educators have long been anxious over the implications of widespread federal aid to education. A few institutions for this reason have refused to accept federal subsidies for fear of possible federal "strings" attached to them. There is always the possibility that federal controls over schools and colleges will stem from what Justice McReynolds once described as "seductive benefits" too favorable to be refused.

c. *Corporation Aid*

Aid to education by big business poses further problems in this area. This is a recent development. Only within the past two or three years has the legal right of a corporation to contribute to a college or university been recognized. So far this program of support for education has rested on a sound basis. Industry appears willing to repay part of its obligations to the schools and universities from which it draws most of its trained personnel. So far there has appeared no evidence of any attempts to exert any pressure which could threaten academic freedom. This program of corporation support, however, sets the stage for possible pressures, and colleges and universities may well keep their fingers crossed.

d. *Private Donors—Both Alumni and Others*

Any fund-raising officer of an educational institution will describe, with tears in his eyes, gifts which the college did not get because of the radical or subversive activities of Professor X. Why doesn't the university fire Professor X? This whole issue was brought into the open not long ago in the interchange between Senator Frank Ober (of Ober law fame in Maryland) and Harvard. Mr. Ober wrote to the Harvard Law School that he would give it no money until two Harvard professors charged with Communist affiliations had been dismissed. The reply of Mr. Grenville Clark, for the Harvard Law School alumni, is a classic statement: "But it is also true, I am sure you will agree, that Harvard cannot be influenced at all to depart from her basic tradition of freedom by fear that any gifts will be withheld." Harvard is, however, one of our wealthiest universities and can perhaps more easily afford to resist such pressures than could many other poorer universities.

8. Impact on Academic Freedom of Outside Pressure Groups

Educational institutions, especially those which are tax-supported, are peculiarly vulnerable to the campaigns of pressure groups. This is probably natural in view of the deep community interest in the public schools and the corresponding sense of community responsibility for them.

The impact of these pressures is widespread. It reaches the teaching staff, outside speakers, the use of educational buildings by minority groups, textbooks, libraries, and publications both by student and faculty.

These pressure groups fall into several categories: There are, first, civic community groups which take on the supervision of school activities as a "project" or as part of a broader program. Secondly, there are patriotic organizations which feel that as good citizens they must help save our schools and colleges from Communist and other "undesirable" infiltration. An example of the activities of this kind of group is seen in the long-continuing conflict between the American Legion and Sarah Lawrence College. A number of patriotic groups devote themselves to stamping out what they regard as un-American influences in American education. Third, there are professional groups which do the job commercially. The private purges conducted by these people who make their living hunting Communists will be dealt with more fully later. *(Infra, p. 201.)*

Academic freedom is also stoutly defended by private pressure groups. Some posts of the American Legion have protested against assaults on academic freedom. The alumni of colleges and universities are by no means inactive in defense of freedom on the campus. Finally, there are influential private groups devoted solely to the protection of academic freedom. Of these the American Association of University Professors is the most notable and successful.

SELECTED READINGS

Under the auspices of the American Academic Freedom Project at Columbia University two notable studies have recently emerged: Richard Hofstadter and Walter P. Metzger, *The Development of Academic Freedom in the United States* (New York: Columbia University Press, 1955), which is a historical study; and Robert M. MacIver, *Academic Freedom in Our Time* (New York: Columbia University Press, 1955), which deals with current problems. Other books reflecting varying viewpoints are: William F. Buckley, Jr., *God and Man at Yale* (Chicago: Henry Regnery, 1951); Russell Kirk, *Academic Freedom: An Essay in Definition* (Chicago: Henry Regnery, 1955); Harold Taylor, *On Education and Freedom* (New York: Abelard-Schumann, 1954); Sidney Hook, *Heresy, Yes—Conspiracy, No* (New York: John Day, 1953); Norman Thomas, *The Test of Freedom* (New York: Norton, 1954); E. Merrill Root, *Collectivism on the Campus* (New York: Devin-Adair, 1955).

ACADEMIC FREEDOM 91

Conflicting viewpoints on the dismissal in 1948 of certain Communist professors at the University of Washington are presented in: *Communism and Academic Freedom: The Record of the Tenure Cases at the University of Washington* (Seattle: University of Washington Press, 1949); and Vern Countryman, *Un-American Activities in the State of Washington: The Work of the Canwell Committee* (Ithaca: Cornell University Press, 1951).

Committees of Congress have from time to time investigated and reported upon alleged subversive influences in schools and colleges. See, for example, *Subversive Influence in the Educational Process,* Report of Sub-Committee of Committee on Judiciary, United States Senate, 83d Cong., 1st Sess., July 17, 1953 (preceded by hearings).

E. Edmund Reuter, Jr., *The School Administration and Subversive Activities—A Study of the Administration of Restraints on Alleged Subversive Activities of Public School Personnel* (New York: Bureau of Publications, Teachers College, Columbia University, 1951), compiles and analyzes measures aimed at disloyal public school personnel.

American Association of University Professors Bulletin (Easton, Pa., quarterly), devotes much of its space to problems of academic freedom on the college and university level.

· III ·

Freedom of Religion: Separation of Church and State

A. PROTECTION OF RELIGIOUS OPINION FROM GOVERNMENTAL ABRIDGMENT

The First and Fourteenth Amendments protect the freedom of religion against governmental abridgment and interference. The problems posed here fall into a number of groups:

1. RELIGIOUS FREEDOM NOT A PROTECTION OF ANTISOCIAL CONDUCT

The religious liberty which is protected by the Constitution is essentially freedom of religious thought and expression; it does not include conduct which violates the criminal law, offends public morals, or interferes with the legitimate exercise of the police power for the protection of public safety and health. This has been the interpretation since 1878, when the Supreme Court refused to allow a Mormon polygamist to defend himself against a criminal charge on the basis of his religion. *(Reynolds* v. *United States,* 98 U.S. 145.) Issues of this general sort continue to arise.

Professional faith-healing has been made illegal in some states in the Union. Cases involving it continue to crop up. In 1944 the federal government prosecuted one Ballard for using the mails to defraud in advertising his ability to heal by mail. The Supreme Court held that to conform to the First Amendment the jury could pass only on whether Ballard sincerely believed that he had supernatural powers and not on whether the jury believed he had. *(United States* v. *Ballard,* 322 U.S. 78.)

Lawful health requirements must prevail over religious objection. There is no new principle here. In 1951 an RH baby in Chicago was taken from its parents who were Jehovah's Witnesses and, over their protests, was given a blood transfusion. In 1952 a Christian Scientist, a student at the University of Washington, was required to have a chest X-ray in order to remain in the university. Both actions were sustained in the courts. *(People* ex rel. *Wallace* v. *Labrenz,* 411 Ill. 618, 1952; certiorari denied, 344 U.S. 824, 1952; *State* ex rel. *Holcomb* v. *Armstrong,* 39 Wash. 2d 860, 1952.) Part of the opposition to the current drive to bring about the fluoridation of public water supplies comes from Christian Scientists, who object on the ground that this is medication. Their objections will doubtless not prevail, though it is probable that a Christian Scientist could not be compelled to drink fluoridated water against his will.

In 1946 the Mann Act, which prohibits transporting women in interstate commerce for immoral purposes, was enforced against a Mormon polygamist who took an extra wife over a state line. The Supreme Court upheld his conviction. (*Cleveland* v. *United States*, 329 U.S. 14, 1946.) In 1954 the state of Arizona moved against a polygamist colony; a critical problem arising from this action was the rather complicated one concerning the custody of children born in families practicing polygamy.

2. "Preferred Status" Accorded to Religious Belief and Its Expression

Beginning in the forties, Supreme Court decisions have given broader protection against governmental restraints on modes of religious expression than they have extended to nonreligious expression. Concretely, Jehovah's Witnesses who engage in canvassing and doorbell ringing for the purpose of distributing religious literature have been held exempt from licensing and from some of the other controls which are imposed upon those who sell magazines or other merchandise.

3. Conscientious Objectors

Technically, conscientious objectors enjoy no constitutional rights in support of their position of resistance to law and the demands of government; nevertheless our national self-respect does not allow us to condone brutal and inhumane treatment to persons who take this position on grounds of conscience. There have been a number of developments in the field of the rights of conscientious objectors:

a. *Civilian Rights*

In the area of civilian rights conscientious objectors won a notable victory in the Supreme Court decision in 1946 *(Girouard* v. *United States,* 328 U.S. 61) which reversed three earlier decisions *(Schwimmer* v. *United States,* 279 U.S. 644, 1929; *Macintosh* v. *United States,* 283 U.S. 605, 1931; *United States* v. *Bland,* 283 U.S. 636, 1931) and granted American citizenship to one Girouard, who was unwilling to fight in the United States army but was willing to engage in noncombatant service. In 1949 citizenship was given to a man who would not serve in the army at all. *(Cohnstaedt* v. *Immigration and Naturalization Service,* 339 U.S. 901.) In 1950 a statute was passed which required, as part of the new citizen's oath of allegiance, a declaration of willingness to bear arms; but the statute contained an exception with respect to conscientious objectors. In the McCarran-Walter Immigration and Nationality Act of 1952, Congress added the "Supreme Being clause," which recognizes conscientious objection only upon the part of those who recognize a Supreme Being; it also required the conscientious objector to agree to do civilian work. Thus this Act barred from citizenship both nonreligious and absolutist objectors (those who resist not only military service but all conscripted service as well). In the same year Congress provided that a person may lose his citizenship for leaving the country for the purpose of avoiding military duty.

In 1945 a conscientious objector was barred in Illinois from the practice of law on the ground that he could not honestly take the required oath to support the Illinois constitution because one clause of it called for compulsory duty in the National Guard; the Supreme Court of the United

States held that due process was not denied in this case. (*In re Summers*, 325 U.S. 561.)

Recently a conscientious objector refused to join a labor union on the ground that his religious beliefs forbade his membership. He lost his job as a result, and the question whether his dismissal is valid under the National Labor Relations Act has still not been decided.

Conscientious objectors have been subjected to very few forms of discrimination. The Atomic Energy Commission does not regard a man who is a conscientious objector on nonreligious grounds as a good security risk. In Oklahoma the adjutant of the National Guard refused to allow Jehovah's Witnesses to meet in the state armory because their religious beliefs were hostile to those of the National Guard. There have been, however, no loyalty oath requirements directed at conscientious objectors, with the exception of the Oklahoma oath which was held invalid on other grounds. (*Wieman* v. *Updegraff*, 344 U.S. 183, 1952.)

b. *Military Rights*

Problems concerning conscientious objectors continue to arise under military conscription statutes. Recent developments here are as follows:

(1) *Holdovers from World War II.* Six thousand conscientious objectors were sent to prison during World War II (more than two-thirds were Jehovah's Witnesses), thereby becoming felons and as such subject to heavy civil and political disabilities; in some states felons are barred from various professions, denied drivers' licenses, and required to register and report. Efforts to secure a general presidential amnesty for this group have failed. President Truman pardoned fifteen hundred persons convicted under the Selective Service Act, but not all of these were conscientious

objectors. (There were altogether fifteen thousand violators of the law including the six thousand conscientious objectors.)

(2) *Universal Military Training and Service Act of 1948.* This included a "Supreme Being clause." The 1940 statute had recognized conscientious objection based upon "religious training and belief." The new Act added that "religious training and belief in this connection means an individual's belief in relation to a Supreme Being involving duties superior to those arising from any human relation, but does not include essentially political, sociological, or philosophical views or a mere personal moral code." This definition narrowed substantially the group of conscientious objectors accorded concessions under the Selective Service Act of 1940.

(3) *The Selective Service Act of 1951.* The 1948 statute simply deferred the conscientious objector to IV-E status, but in 1951 the law was changed and required two years of civilian work in an approved government or nonprofit agency. This of course denied any recognition to the absolutists (those who will not co-operate at all and many of whom will not even register under the Act). Most of the conscientious objectors employed under the Act of 1951 have received pay for their work, although there has been some discrimination against them.

(4) *Supreme Court decisions.* Conscientious objector status has been improved as a result of several Supreme Court decisions. In 1946 in the Estep case *(Estep* v. *United States,* 327 U.S. 114) the Court held that a draft board order was subject to a limited amount of judicial review for the purpose of guaranteeing that it was not wholly arbitrary. Prior to this, the draft board's discretion had been prac-

tically uncontrolled. In 1953 in the Nugent case *(United States* v. *Nugent,* 346 U.S. 1) the Court held that where FBI reports are relied upon in an appeal hearing on the status of a conscientious objector the conscientious objector is entitled to "a fair résumé" of the adverse evidence in such reports. In 1955 in the Simmons case *(Simmons* v. *United States,* 348 U.S. 397) the Court reinforced this by holding that the conscientious objector is entitled to such a résumé, not as a matter of grace, but as a right. Several lower courts have held that FBI reports in these hearings must actually be produced in order that the fairness of the résumé may be evaluated; but the Department of Justice has refused to allow this and has dropped some prosecutions rather than do so.

In 1953 in the Dickinson case *(Dickinson* v. *United States,* 346 U.S. 389) the Court held that a draft board's conclusion that a conscientious objector is lying must be supported by at least some evidence, not merely the board's belief. In 1955 in the Sicurella case *(Sicurella* v. *United States,* 348 U.S. 385) the Court held that Jehovah's Witnesses are conscientious objectors within the meaning of the statute; this was held in spite of the contention that Jehovah's Witnesses do not oppose all wars, but would fight in a religious war, such as the Battle of Armageddon.

(5) *Repeated prosecutions of conscientious objectors.* It is obvious that both the nonreligious conscientious objectors and the absolutists are bound to go to prison. Thirteen have been convicted a second time after having served prison sentences. One man served eighteen months in civilian work during World War II, served a prison sentence in World War II, and has served two prison sentences under the Act of 1948. It would appear that the law permits

the government to keep the persistent conscientious objector in prison for the rest of his life if it so desires.

(6) *Status of counselors to conscientious objectors.* In a limited number of cases persons who have counseled or advised conscientious objectors not to register or otherwise comply with the Selective Service Act have been convicted under the statute.

(7) *Record of armed services attitude.* The record indicates that the armed forces have been careful to observe the provisions of the law with respect to conscientious objectors. There has been special caution to avoid compelling conscientious objectors to undergo training with weapons. Since there is no provision for the discharge of conscientious objectors from the army after they get in it, a number of them have been subject to court martial when found to fall within reach of the law.

(8) *Prison treatment.* With an isolated exception or two there is no record that conscientious objectors in prison have been in any way discriminated against or mistreated.

B. SEPARATION OF CHURCH AND STATE

The First Amendment not only forbids Congress to prohibit the free exercise of religion, it also forbids Congress to make any law "respecting an establishment of religion" —a clause designed to guarantee the separation of church and state.

While Congress itself has passed no law which could be seriously interpreted as an establishment of religion (see, however, instances of "recognition" of religion, *infra,* p. 106), there has been a series of important cases dealing with religion in the public schools in which the Supreme Court has held that the establishment-of-religion clause is also a restriction upon the states by reason of its inclusion in the due process clause of the Fourteenth Amendment, and it has proceeded to say what that clause means.

The problems raised here fall into three groups: The first group comprises the issues raised by various forms of aid extended by state and local governments to parochial schools or parochial school children; these have become increasingly pressing as a result of the spread of parochial schools and the generally increasing influence of the Catholic Church in American communities. The second group is concerned with religious instruction and ceremonies in the public schools. The third group is concerned with the mergers of sectarian schools with public schools.

1. State Aid to Parochial Schools

In 1930 the Supreme Court held that the state of Louisiana could validly provide free textbooks to all school children in the state including parochial school children. (*Cochran* v. *Louisiana State Board of Education,* 281 U.S. 370.) To do so was a service to the school child, not to the school which he attended, and did not deny due process of law by spending tax money for a private purpose. The establishment-of-religion clause had not been assimiliated, at this time, into the Fourteenth Amendment as a limitation on the states.

a. *The "Child Benefit Doctrine"*

In 1947 the case of *Everson* v. *Board of Education* (330 U.S. 1) reached the Supreme Court and attracted nationwide attention. The issue here was whether a New Jersey town could spend tax funds for free bus transportation for parochial as well as for public school children. In a five-to-four decision the Court held this spending to be valid on the ground that the payments were an aid, not to religion, but to the children. This doctrine has been dubbed "the child benefit theory."

In the Everson case the Court was unanimous in stating that the states are forbidden to extend aid to religion directly or indirectly. It spoke of the wall of separation between church and state created by the First Amendment and made applicable to the states through the Fourteenth Amendment. The Justices all agreed that government could not aid religion. They disagreed on whether, in this particular case, religion was being aided.

The child benefit theory has plausibility, but it leaves many problems unsolved which will ultimately come to the Court. If it benefits the child and not the school to give him free textbooks and free bus rides, does it also benefit the child and not the school to give him free nursing, medical service, cafeterias, swimming pools, and other advantages calling for heavy capital expenditures? At just what point does aid to the child become so substantial as to be aid to religion?

The opinions in the Everson case brought bitter protests even from those who agreed with the result. The Catholic hierarchy, as well as a number of respected students of constitutional law, challenged the Court's interpretation that the First Amendment required a complete and absolute ban upon all aid to religion. It was argued that the establishment clause was intended merely to guarantee equality of treatment among religious groups, and not to bar any and all governmental aid to religion.

A question posed by the Everson case is whether, in view of the fact that the local school board "may" provide free bus transportation for parochial school students, such students may not validly claim this service under the equal protection clause whether or not the school board is willing to give it.

2. Religious Instruction in Public Schools

The problems of religious instruction and religious ceremonies in the public schools are very old ones. There has been a long and steady trend toward eliminating religious instruction and religious control from the public schools, although the Supreme Court in 1925 *(Pierce v. Society of Sisters,* 268 U.S. 510) held that the Fourteenth Amendment guaranteed to parents the right to send their children to parochial or other nonpublic schools if such schools met the educational standards set up by the state.

a. *The "Released-Time Program"*

To what extent, if any, can religion validly be made a part of the public school curriculum? It is felt in many communities that some sort of systematic religious instruction should be made available to school children. From this has emerged the so-called "released-time program," whereby public school children whose parents approve are excused from their regular studies for a fixed period so that they may attend religious classes taught by teachers drawn from the various religious denominations. Pupils not attending these classes pursue regular school work during this period.

A released-time program set up in Champaign, Illinois, was held by the Supreme Court of the United States in 1948 to extend aid to religion and therefore to be a violation of the Fourteenth Amendment. *(McCollum v. Board of Education,* 333 U.S. 203.) Under this program school children were released for an hour a week from regular school duties to take classes in religious instruction. The classes were held in the school buildings, attendance records were kept, and the administrative machinery of the school system was employed to make the program effective. The Court held that the use of school property and the tax-supported school machinery amounted to an unconstitutional grant of aid to religion.

In 1952 a released-time program in New York was upheld by the Supreme Court of the United States. *(Zorach v. Clauson,* 343 U.S. 306.) Under the New York plan, children were excused from school with their parents' consent for the purpose of going to neighboring churches or other places where religious instruction was carried on, and those who did not go to the religious classes were kept in school to study. A divided Court (six to three), held that this did not constitute enough aid to religion to violate the Fourteenth Amendment. Dissenting Justices strongly urged that the plan depended entirely for its operation upon the compulsion and discipline of the school system, since the children were "released" rather than "dismissed."

b. *Bible Reading*

The problem of Bible reading in the public schools was dealt with in 1950 by the Supreme Court of New Jersey. *(Doremus v. Board of Education,* 5 N.J. 435; appeal dismissed, 342 U.S. 429, 1952.) Here was involved a state requirement that a certain number of verses from the Old Testament together with the Lord's Prayer be read at the opening of the school day. This was attacked as a form of religious teaching and indoctrination. The New Jersey court held that the Old Testament and Lord's Prayer were not "sectarian" and therefore did not comprise the kind of religious instruction which is forbidden by the Constitution; the court spoke of the importance of religion in fighting atheistic communism and suggested that the religious ceremonies might be regarded as in aid of a public purpose. The state courts are divided on the issue of Bible reading. Of some eighteen decisions, the ratio is two to one in favor of the validity of the practice.

In 1953 the Supreme Court of New Jersey held that the Fourteenth Amendment forbade the Gideon Society to give to school children the King James Protestant version of the New Testament. (*Tudor* v. *Board of Education,* 14 N.J. 31.) (The Bibles were to be given only if the parents of the children consented.) The court held that the King James Bible was a sectarian book, a view vigorously supported by Catholics and Jews, and therefore that this did amount to forbidden religious instruction. It is not easy to reconcile the two New Jersey cases, and neither case was reviewed by the Supreme Court of the United States on the merits.

3. Mergers of Sectarian and Public Schools

Possibly the most acute problem affecting religion in the public schools is a regional problem and one not much known outside the areas in which it exists. In a substantial number of communities, largely in the middle west, parochial schools have been assimilated into the public school system and receive direct tax support. In some cases the tax-supported parochial school is the only one. This is not a new development. It reaches back, in fact, as far as the nineties, when the "Faribault plan" was put into operation.

Under this plan Catholic schools were incorporated into the public school system, though there was a vague understanding that the Catholic schools would be secularized—an understanding which was never complied with. There are at present some four hundred school systems under this plan.

One or two aspects of this problem should be emphasized:

First, this practice was well established long before the states, through the assimilation of the First Amendment into the Fourteenth Amendment, were held to be barred by the federal Constitution from giving financial aid to religion if they wanted to do so.

Second, in many of the communities involved the population is overwhelmingly Catholic, and there is often no minority group sufficiently disturbed by the arrangement to start a legal attack upon it.

In the third place, there are communities in which Protestant parents, bitterly resentful but practically helpless, are compelled to send their children to Catholic schools since the communities have provided no tax-supported nonsectarian schools.

This direct violation of the First Amendment ban upon aid to religion has been stricken down in most of the states in which cases involving it have been brought to the courts. These decisions, however, have not brought about statewide compliance with the courts' decrees.

In a number of communities Catholic teachers have been employed in the public schools and have worn religious garb while teaching. There has been opposition to this, and in a number of cases the state courts have ordered the practice abandoned.

4. Miscellaneous Governmental Recognitions of Religion

a. *In the Schools*

Controversy broke out in New York City when the Board of Education ordered the deletion of certain material taught in courses in health and hygiene in order to avoid offending Christian Scientists, and in 1951 a New York statute excused students from courses in hygiene which conflict with their religion. Even more controversy arose when the New York Board of Regents "authorized" the opening of school sessions with a nonsectarian prayer. Objection to this was so bitter that the Board of Education in New York City watered down the suggestion by requiring simply the singing of the fourth stanza of "America." Over against this official recognition of religion may be placed the banning by an assistant school superintendent in Brooklyn in 1947 of the singing of Christmas carols in the public schools. One may note also the action taken by the New York City authorities in dropping from all school libraries the magazine *The Nation,* because it had printed Paul Blanshard's articles criticizing the Catholic church.

b. *General*

Back in 1844 Justice Story remarked, "The Christian religion is part of the common law." *(Vidal* v. *Girard's Executors,* 2 Howard 127.) It is true that government on all levels—federal, state, and local—continues to recognize religion in a wide range of ceremonials and practices. The more recent developments in this area are the following:

The Christian Sunday continues to be protected by law as it has been over the years. In 1951 the Supreme Court refused to review a New York decision upholding the conviction under the New York statute of orthodox Jews for the crime of performing certain kinds of work on Sunday. (*Friedman* v. *New York*, 341 U.S. 907.)

In 1952 President Truman aroused a storm of protest and controversy by appointing an ambassador to the Vatican. Protestant objection to this was based in part on the allegation that this was a recognition of religion. Some scholars take the position that the First Amendment provision forbidding religious establishments applies only to Congress and not to the President.

In 1954 the United States Information Agency created the position of "Chief of Religious Information," and a distinguished clergyman was appointed to this post. This action was attacked as a violation of the First Amendment.

In 1954 Congress passed a statute amending the Pledge of Allegiance to the United States so that it contains the phrase "this nation under God."

SELECTED READINGS

An exhaustive historical and analytical treatment of religious liberty and the separation of church and state is Anson Phelps Stokes, *Church and State in the United States*, 3 vols. (New York: Harper, 1950). Less extensive, but highly valuable, is Leo Pfeffer, *Church, State and Freedom* (Boston: Beacon Press, 1953). An older but useful book is William George Torpey, *Judicial Doctrines of Religious Rights in America* (Chapel Hill: University of North Carolina Press, 1948). The more important judicial decisions in this field are compiled in Mark DeWolfe Howe, *Cases on Church and State in the United States* (Cambridge: Harvard University Press, 1952).

The controversy over religion in the public schools has produced a literature of its own, much of it strongly argumentative. For the more objective studies, see Alvin W. Johnson and Frank H. Yost, *Separation of Church and State in the United States* (Minneapolis: University of Minnesota Press, 1948), as well as the sections in Leo Pfeffer's book (just mentioned). For a vigorous statement of the Catholic position on these issues see James M. O'Neill, *Religion and Education under the Constitution* (New York: Harper, 1949). Vashti McCollum, *One Woman's Fight* (Boston: Beacon Press, 1951), is a colorful story of the McCollum case written by its central figure.

Mulford Q. Sibley and Philip E. Jacob, *Conscription of Conscience—The American State and the Conscientious Objector 1940–1947* (Ithaca: Cornell University Press, 1952), presents the record and discusses the problems of the conscientious objector in World War II.

· IV ·

The Right to Security and Freedom of the Person

A. THE RIGHT OF HABEAS CORPUS

THE writ of habeas corpus, an ancient and valued bulwark of personal liberty, is the device by which a person restrained of his liberty gets from a judge a prompt decision on the legality of his imprisonment. The right exists in all the states, while the United States Constitution assumes its existence in federal courts by rigidly limiting the circumstances under which "the privilege of the writ of habeas corpus" may be suspended. Federal statutes and rules regarding habeas corpus are highly technical and cannot be discussed here. Habeas corpus differs, however, from an appeal, since it does not provide for a review of errors in the record but is confined to the basic question of the legality of the imprisonment.

1. Federal Habeas Corpus for Prisoners Held under State Authority

The doctrine of the "supremacy of national law" prevents a state judge from issuing a writ of habeas corpus on behalf of a federal prisoner. But the converse is not true. In 1867 Congress provided explicitly that the writ should extend to all persons restrained of their liberty in violation of the Constitution or a law or treaty of the United States, and it required the federal court to ascertain the facts and to "dispose of the party as law and justice require." This clearly authorized federal habeas corpus action to determine whether a state prisoner is being denied his federal rights.

This federal discipline of state courts through habeas corpus has recently generated considerable state resentment, and civil liberty issues are raised by proposals that federal judicial authority in the area be curbed. There have been a substantial number of these habeas corpus cases. For some time the Supreme Court has been applying its doctrine that the due process clause of the Fourteenth Amendment requires a "fair trial" in a state court. (*Infra*, p. 156.) One of the elements of a "fair trial" is the right of counsel whenever essential justice requires it, and the Supreme Court during the last twenty years has granted relief to a number of state prisoners who had been denied counsel. The result has been a flow of petitions to federal courts for habeas corpus on behalf of state convicts, some of whom had been in prison for long periods of time, alleging that they had been denied counsel at the time of their conviction. In 1954 a federal district judge in Chicago released on habeas corpus Roger (The Terrible) Touhy, the prohibition-era gangster who had served twenty years of a ninety-nine-year sentence for kidnaping, on the ground that he had been convicted by perjured testimony (which would, of course, be a denial of due process). A federal circuit judge returned him to prison, pending review by an appellate court.

Judges of state supreme courts which have carefully reviewed the constitutionality of these state convictions are naturally offended at being overruled by a federal district judge. As the chief justice of the Supreme Court of Massachusetts said: "One single federal judge can upset the whole applecart. That is not right." Federal judges are themselves not happy over the situation. Most of them do not enjoy overriding state supreme courts. In 1954 the chief justices of the forty-eight states unanimously endorsed an amendment to the federal statutes which would deprive lower federal courts of power to nullify state court judgments in criminal cases. Their contention is that only the Supreme Court should do this, and should do it only under conditions much more restricted than at present. A similar proposal has been approved by a committee of the Judicial Conference of the United States composed of federal judges.

This proposed concession to the dignity and authority of state courts is strongly opposed by some on the ground that there is a long and sordid record of denial of due process of law in the courts of a number of states and that ultimate relief through habeas corpus in a federal court after every other procedure has been exhausted ought not to be cut off. It is also pointed out that there has been no "jail delivery" under the Habeas Corpus Act and that the number of cases involved is very small indeed.

2. Suspension of the Writ of Habeas Corpus

The Constitution provides that the writ of habeas corpus shall not be suspended "unless when in cases of rebellion or invasion the public safety may require it." Congress early gave to the President the authority to decide when these emergencies exist, as well as power to suspend the writ. When the President has suspended the writ of habeas corpus, he has done so by declaring martial law to replace normal civil authority, as in Hawaii during World War II. Civil liberties are abridged, in fact they are blotted out, by such action; but the problems incident to martial law are beyond the scope of this analysis.

B. FREEDOM OF MOVEMENT AND RESIDENCE

1. Freedom of Movement within the Country

As early as 1868 the Supreme Court held *(Crandall* v. *Nevada,* 6 Wallace 35) that it is a privilege of national citizenship to travel freely across state lines without interference from any state; in this case Nevada had imposed a tax on the privilege. In *Edwards* v. *California* (314 U.S. 160, 1941), the Supreme Court agreed unanimously in invalidating a California statute, similar to those of more than twenty other states, which penalized the bringing into the state of indigent persons. The majority of the Court held that the California statute was an invalid state burden on interstate commerce; but Justice Robert Jackson in a concurring opinion persuasively argued that it was also an abridgment of the rights of national citizenship. He said:

This court should, however, hold squarely that it is a privilege of citizenship of the United States, protected from state abridgment, to enter any state of the Union, either for temporary sojourn or for the establishment of permanent residence therein and for gaining resultant citizenship thereof. If national citizenship means less than this, it means nothing.

It is clear that this freedom of movement does not extend to various groups of persons placed under legal restraint.

Here would be listed persons subject to the draft (who are not allowed to leave the country), persons on bail or parole, enemy aliens in time of war, and aliens on limited visas. No civil liberty issue seems to be involved here as long as the restrictions imposed are reasonable and not arbitrary. It is urged that civil liberty problems have arisen in connection with the government's mode of dealing with some persons being held for deportation to countries which, because of war or other international complications, cannot or will not receive them.

A bizarre and obviously rare type of state restriction upon freedom of movement was the decree of "banishment" issued in 1948 by a Connecticut court. A man charged with an assault with intent to commit murder was acquitted on grounds of insanity and committed to a state hospital. He was released by the judge on condition that he post a $5,000 bond and that he "leave the territorial limits of the state of Connecticut forever." He was also required to notify the county attorney of his whereabouts each month. It would seem that to give a man the equivalent of a suspended sentence on condition that he leave the state poses a number of constitutional and civil liberty questions. The persons affected are not, however, likely to raise them for obvious reasons.

2. Freedom to Leave the Country—The Right to a Passport

Before World War I American citizens traveled freely the world over without passports. Passports were available upon request, but were not required in order to leave the country. Increasing world tensions thereafter led most foreign countries to require an American citizen to have an

American passport, and our own government took the position that in a declared state of emergency (in force since 1941) an American citizen could not travel abroad without a passport. The Immigration and Nationality Act of 1952 makes it a crime to do so in these circumstances. In 1926 Congress had provided that the Secretary of State "may" issue passports under regulations set up by the President; the President thereupon issued regulations authorizing the Secretary of State to issue, deny, or invalidate passports "in his discretion."

This theory of unlimited executive discretion over the issuance of passports no doubt stems from the doctrine of the government's unlimited authority in the field of foreign affairs. Be that as it may, the State Department readily accepted the idea that it had complete discretion in the matter of passports and that this relieved it of any procedural requirements as well as any duty to explain why it denied or revoked a passport in any specific case. The Internal Security Act of 1950 forbade the granting of a passport to a member of a "Communist-action" organization, as defined in the Act. The State Department, in 1952, in regulations designed to "enforce the spirit" of the Internal Security Act, proceeded to deny passports not only to Communists but also to persons "suspected of furthering the Communist cause."

There ensued after 1950 the denial or invalidating of passports by the State Department with only the bare explanation that "travel abroad at this time would be contrary to the best interest of the United States." The Department reported in May, 1952, that during the preceding year it had barred three hundred citizens from going abroad. The Department's action in many of these cases

SECURITY OF THE PERSON

brought substantial protest. The issue was sharply dramatized by the denial of a passport in February, 1952, to Dr. Linus Pauling, world-renowned chemist at the California Institue of Technology and Nobel Prize winner. Dr. Pauling was told that his proposed trip to London to attend a scientific conference would not be "in the best interests of the United States." He learned after persistent inquiry that this was because he was "suspected" of Communist sympathies, although the Department could not tell him (for security reasons) the basis of these suspicions. In July, after an almost nation-wide protest, Dr. Pauling received his passport upon signing a statement that he was not, and never had been, a Communist, a statement he had offered to sign in the first place.

To meet mounting criticism, the Department of State in 1952 set up a Board of Passport Appeals to review rulings by the Passport Division. The Board was to make its own rules of procedure, but the right to a hearing and representation of counsel was assured, as well as a transcript of the applicant's own testimony. Recourse to the Board, however, was denied to those who would not make an affidavit denying present and past Communist membership. The denial of passports on the ground of the political views and affiliations of the applicant continued.

It had long been assumed that there was no judicial control over the discretionary handling of passports by the State Department. In 1952, however, in *Bauer* v. *Acheson,* (106 Fed. Supp. 445), a three-judge district court in the District of Columbia held that due process requires notice and hearing before a passport can be revoked or before its renewal can be refused. The State Department, however, was not alert to the judicial storm warning. Dr. Otto Nathan, internationally known economist and executor of the will of Albert Einstein, had been trying without success to get a passport since 1952. In June, 1955, the United States District Court in the District of Columbia ordered the State Department to issue a passport to Dr. Nathan under pain of contempt. *(Nathan v. Dulles,* 129 Fed. Supp. 951.) On appeal, the Court of Appeals of the District ordered the Department to give Dr. Nathan a "quasi-judicial" hearing at which it must present evidence in support of its denial of his passport and at which he would be able to reply. *(Dulles v. Nathan,* 225 Fed. 2d 29.) Without complying with the Court's order, the Department gave Dr. Nathan his passport forthwith. Two weeks later came the decision of the Court of Appeals in the District of Columbia in the Schachtman case. *(Schachtman v. Dulles,* 225 Fed. 2d 938, 1955.) Schachtman had been trying for three and a half years to get a passport but had been refused because he was a member of the Independent Socialist League, a Trotzkyite group, which had been listed as subversive by the Attorney General. Rejecting entirely the State Department's claim that the issuance of passports is a matter within its "exclusive control," the Court of Appeals of the District declared that the right of an American citizen to travel abroad is a "natural right" and that the Department may not refuse to give him a passport on grounds which do not meet the test of due process of law. Schachtman received his passport, and in August the Department announced that it would not appeal the decision in the Schachtman case.

C. PROTECTION AGAINST SLAVERY AND PEONAGE

While slavery as a social institution was ended at the close of the Civil War, remnants of it, and ingenious variations of it, still crop up, and there is continuing need for the Thirteenth Amendment, which reads: "Neither slavery nor involuntary servitude, except as a punishment for crime whereof the party shall have been duly convicted, shall exist within the United States, or any place subject to their jurisdiction. Congress shall have power to enforce this Article by appropriate legislation." This is the only civil liberty provision in the Constitution which directly applies to the conduct of private persons rather than that of governments. Congress has implemented the Amendment by statutes which define and punish the crimes of slavery and peonage.

1. SLAVERY

The crime of holding another in slavery is naturally very rare, but it does occur. In 1947 in the Ingalls case *(United States v. Ingalls,* 73 Fed. Supp. 76) a woman was convicted of having held a maidservant in a state of slavery for some twenty-five years; the servant was unpaid, and she was kept from leaving the household by threats by her mistress to disclose certain misconduct of the servant which had occurred nearly forty years earlier. In 1954 two brothers in Alabama were convicted in a federal court of having held two Negroes in slavery.

2. PEONAGE

Peonage is involuntary servitude based upon real or alleged debt. It is most likely to be found where ignorant laborers, usually agricultural, are employed on a large scale. Negroes and Mexican laborers have been its special victims in the South and Southwest.

Several southern states attempted to make peonage legally possible by the device of making it a crime (fraud) for any person to whom an advance of wages has been made to leave his job before the money is either earned or repaid. Under such a law a southern plantation owner could advance a few dollars to his Negro laborers when he hired them, keep them continually in his debt, and thus create a situation in which the laborer became in reality a peon. The laborer never worked out his debt, and he became a criminal if he quit his job before he did so. The Supreme Court has been very tough in striking down subterfuges of this sort. *Pollock* v. *Williams* (322 U.S. 4, 1944), a Florida case, is the last of a series of decisions which have held that such provisions create conditions of peonage.

In 1947 the Civil Rights Section in the Department of Justice (discussed *infra,* p. 125) learned that local officers in a Georgia county were arresting and imprisoning persons under the terms of the labor contract law already held invalid by the Supreme Court in *Taylor v. Georgia* (315 U.S. 25, 1942). After conference with the local officials the practice was abandoned.

Ingenious attempts are still made by employers in some parts of the country to continue peonage. Thus a warrant may be issued charging some imaginary crime, and the worker may be either arrested and put in jail or returned to work on the employer's farm. Some employers have sought to use the federal Fugitive Felon Act of 1934, which makes it a crime for a fugitive from justice to travel in interstate commerce, as a means of getting back laborers who have quit and left the state. A case is reported of a plantation owner from Georgia who came to Chicago armed with warrants under this statute and accompanied by a deputy sheriff, for the purpose of returning some thirty Negroes who had fled from his plantation. This attempt backfired. The plantation owner was promptly indicted in the federal court in Chicago for violation of the peonage as well as the civil rights statutes. He hurried back home and the federal court in Georgia refused to allow him to be extradited to Illinois for trial. *(United States* v. *Cunningham,* 40 Fed. Supp. 399, 1941.)

A unique application of the peonage statute was upheld in 1946 in the Pierce case. *(Pierce* v. *United States,* 146 Fed. 2d 84; and 157 Fed. 2d 848.) Pierce operated a roadhouse in which girls employed as waitresses and hostesses also acted as prostitutes. By keeping them constantly in debt to him Pierce had been able to prevent their leaving the place. He had been careful not to violate the White Slave Act by bringing any of the girls from across the state line. He was, however, indicted and convicted of peonage. The Supreme Court denied certiorari. (329 U.S. 814, 1947.)

Peonage does not flourish in the open, and its victims are all too often ignorant of their rights and helpless in their own defense. Constant vigilance is needed to ferret out and punish these brutal invasions of personal rights.

The Department of Justice feels that the present laws against peonage contain loopholes which should be plugged. Bills designed to do this were introduced in the Eighty-fourth Congress. The major change proposed would make it a crime to *attempt* to reduce a person to a condition of peonage, as well as actually doing so.

D. PROTECTION AGAINST LYNCHING

Lynching is not a federal crime and there is no universally accepted definition of it. A bill introduced in the House of Representatives in 1955 opens with this "finding":

Lynching is mob violence. It is violence which injures or kills its immediate victims. It is also violence which may be used to terrorize the racial, national, or religious groups of which the victims are members, thereby hindering all members of these groups in the free exercise of the rights guaranteed them by the Constitution and laws of the United States.

There is no state in the Union in which a lynching has not occurred. Most cases have, however, occurred in the southern states, and in most cases Negroes have been the victims. Happily, lynching is disappearing throughout the country. There were 130 lynchings in 1901; in 1950 there were two; in 1951 there was one; there have been none since, although there have been lawless acts of terrorism directed against Negroes, as well as clandestine murders.

1. Lynching as a National Civil Liberty Problem

Although lynching is a crime against the laws of every state in the Union, it has for many years been a major national problem. One reason for this is that many lynchings have had international repercussions. The victims of some of the early lynchings were citizens of foreign nations which violently protested the outrages. The national government was embarrassed at these attempts to hold it internationally liable for crimes against state law over which it had no jurisdiction. Some of the early proposals for federal antilynching legislation would have made it a federal crime to abridge by violence the treaty rights of aliens in this country. The international impact of lynching was made sharply clear during World War II, when news of each lynching was promptly broadcast by German and Japanese radios in their anti-American propaganda.

In addition, certain unique attributes of lynchings, especially in the South, have helped to give them the status of a national problem. Lynchings in the South are usually motivated by racial prejudice, the victims are usually members of a racial minority, and the crime is almost never punished. Southern communities deplore lynchings, but it is almost impossible to get a southern jury to convict a southern white man of the crime. Law enforcement breaks down. This has led to a widespread conviction throughout much of the rest of the country that if the state authorities will not, or cannot, punish those guilty of lynching, the national government ought to take the job over. The President's Committee on Civil Rights in 1947 recommended the enactment of a federal antilynching statute.

2. Methods Proposed for the Federal Control of Lynching

Proposals for the federal control of lynching vary in form, though often all the forms appear in the same bill. The first is to make it a crime to lynch an alien whose treaty rights protect him from violence in this country. Congress may make laws to enforce treaties; ironically, it may thus punish the lynching of a foreigner, while there is sharp dispute over its constitutional power to punish the lynching of an American citizen. A second proposal is to lay a heavy fine upon the local governmental unit in which a lynching occurs and in addition make it liable in damages to the victims of mob violence or to their families. The idea here is to heighten the sense of community responsibility for these outrages. In the third place, punishments are to be imposed upon any state or local official, or anyone acting under color of law, who participates in, aids, or connives at a lynching or fails to make a diligent effort to prevent the lynching of anyone in his custody. One of our present federal civil rights statutes, not limited to lynching, authorizes the punishment of officials in cases of this kind. Finally, on the assumption that there is a federal constitutional right not to be lynched, it is proposed that Congress protect that right by making it a federal crime for *any person* to participate in a lynching.

3. Constitutional Doubts about Federal Control of Lynching

Congress has never passed an antilynching statute, although bills have been before Congress almost constantly since the 1890s. While the bitter political opposition of southern congressmen to such legislation is enough to explain this inaction, it should be made clear that many constitutional lawyers, who would be glad enough on grounds of policy to have Congress pass a broad and effective antilynching statute, believe that Congress does not have the power to do so. Others believe that it has.

This constitutional dispute cannot be aired here, but the main point upon which it turns should be stated. Does the Constitution anywhere give to Congress, directly or by implication, the power to make it a crime for A, a private citizen, to engage in mob violence which results in the lynching of B? Or, does Congress have any more power to punish a lynching in Georgia than to punish a gang murder in Chicago? It is plausibly argued that the Fourteenth Amendment protects a man from being deprived of his life without due process of law; that to lynch a man—particularly if he has been arrested, charged with crime, and is in the custody of the state—is to deprive him of his life without due process of law; and that Congress, which is empowered to enforce the Fourteenth Amendment by legislation, may therefore punish the members of the mob which thus deprived its victim of his life without due process of law. For the most persuasive statement of this argument, see *Ex parte Riggins,* 134 Fed. 404, 1904. It is argued in reply that the Fourteenth Amendment forbids the *states,* not private persons, to deprive persons of their lives without due process; that a mob therefore has not violated and could not violate the Fourteenth Amendment; and Congress, therefore, cannot constitutionally punish what the Amendment does not forbid.

Many feel that Congress could usefully modernize the existing civil rights statutes, which date from the Reconstruction period *(infra,* p. 124), to increase their effectiveness in dealing with state or local officers who are in any way implicated in a lynching. Such officers *are* the *state* within the meaning of the Fourteenth Amendment, their participation in a lynching is *state* deprivation of life without due process of law, and Congress can clearly punish that. It is even proposed that Congress make it a crime for a state official to condone a lynching by not making every diligent effort to protect a prisoner who is in his custody.

E. THE CIVIL RIGHTS SECTION IN THE DEPARTMENT OF JUSTICE

1. Background

Constitutional guarantees of civil liberty are in the main protections which the citizen enjoys against abridgment by the action of government, state or national. No individual can possibly violate the federal Bill of Rights, which begins with the words, "Congress shall make no law," and which has been held to restrict only the federal government. Nor can an individual violate the Fourteenth Amendment, which clearly says "no state" shall do the things forbidden. When the civil liberties of the citizen are interfered with by other individuals, in general it is the state government, not the federal government, which can act to prevent or punish this abuse.

At the same time there are rights and privileges which the citizen enjoys which arise either from the Constitution or from acts of Congress, and Congress may punish individuals who "injure, oppress, threaten, or intimidate any citizen" in the full and free enjoyment of these rights. During the period of Reconstruction, Congress passed a number of laws for the protection of the civil rights of citizens. Some of these were held to be unconstitutional, but two sections remain on the statute books. The first of these punishes "two or more persons who conspire together" to obstruct any citizen in the enjoyment of any right or privilege secured to him by the Constitution or laws of the United States; the second penalizes anyone who "under color of any law, statute, ordinance, regulation or custom, willfully subjects any person to a deprivation of any rights or privileges secured by the Constitution or laws of the United States." These laws have not been modified since they were enacted in 1866 and 1870 respectively. These provisions, together with the statutes on slavery and peonage already discussed, comprise the bulk of the federal government's arsenal of legislation directed against persons who interfere with the civil rights of other persons. The federal statutes authorize civil suits for damages or other relief against public officials or private conspirators who deny or abridge federal rights.

2. Civil Rights Section

The history of federal civil rights legislation well illustrates the truth of the old adage of the common law that "there is no right if there is no remedy." It was not until Attorney General Frank Murphy in 1939 created, in the Criminal Division of the Department of Justice, the Civil Rights Section that any well-planned and imaginative campaign for the effective enforcement of the civil rights statutes was made possible. Prior to the creation of the Section, responsibility for prosecuting persons who violated these statutes rested with the local United States attorneys, and these, especially in southern communities, had displayed little energy or courage in protecting the civil rights of Negroes.

a. *Some Achievements of the Civil Rights Section*

The work of the Section is not widely known, but its achievements have been of real value. Those which relate to civil liberties are as follows:

The Section enforces the slavery and peonage statutes discussed above (p. 117). Here, as in its other work, it relies upon the FBI for investigation and the discovery of evidence. It co-operates with the local United States attorneys in bringing indictments and conducting prosecutions. On occasion it will send its own lawyer to conduct a case.

A common and vicious violation of the Civil Rights Act takes the form of police brutality. The Section has been active in prosecuting these cases and has secured convictions in enough cases to show that it can be done. In 1947 Crews, a town marshall and constable in Florida, arrested a Negro, beat him with a heavy whip, and then compelled him to jump from a high bridge into a river. The Negro was drowned. Crews was indicted under the Civil Rights Act, convicted, and his conviction was sustained in *Crews v. United States* (160 Fed. 2d 746, 1947). In another Florida case a private detective acting as a special police officer was convicted under the Act for physical brutality in extracting a confession from persons suspected of crime. The Supreme Court upheld the conviction. *(Williams v. United States,* 341 U.S. 97, 1951.)

The Civil Rights Section, with the aid of the FBI, has pretty well destroyed the Ku Klux Klan in several states where it was deeply entrenched. The Klan, for its own protection, does not normally indulge in terrorizing acts in its own locality. Rather, its hooded members invade a neighboring state and bring their victims back to the raiders' state for flogging and other mistreatment. The Section has been prosecuting these activities under the Lindbergh Kidnaping Act so successfully that the North Carolina section of the Klan has been broken up. However, in the mounting race tension resulting from the Supreme Court's desegregation decision there has been some evidence of renewed Klan activity in the South.

The Section has made persistent efforts to deal with the

crime of lynching in cases where there is evidence that local officials were implicated in the crime. As we have seen (p. 123), the constitutional authority to prosecute such officers for violation of the Civil Rights Act is clear. The Section has secured indictments in some cases, but, as has been mentioned, it is well nigh impossible to get southern juries to convict in these cases.

The Section has important duties in the enforcement of federal statutes protecting the citizen's right to vote in federal elections. These are usually cases involving discrimination against Negro voters.

b. *Some Frustrations of the Civil Rights Section*

The Civil Rights Section by any reasonable standard would seem to be understaffed for its increasingly important tasks. At present it has eight lawyers and five stenographers, and this has been its customary size. In 1954 the cases referred to it numbered 2,826, while the letters and inquiries received totaled more than ten thousand. In addition to the Section's work that has been described in the preceding pages, it has the duty of enforcing the Hatch Act, the Fair Labor Standards Act, the Safety Appliance Act, the Kickback Act, and the Railway Labor Act. Obviously, from this large volume of business, the Section must select the cases which seem most worth handling and let the rest go. It cannot possibly deal effectively with them all.

The Section is not a division in the Department of Justice, but part of a division. It is responsible directly, not to the Attorney General, but to the Assistant Attorney General who heads the entire Criminal Division. This means that in the matter of administrative supervision, and especially in the matter of the budget, it has small bargaining power and no priorities. It has been rewarded by its superiors for its admirable work by kind words rather than increased appropriations and a larger staff.

c. *Strengthening the Civil Rights Section*

In 1947 the President's Committee on Civil Rights strongly urged the strengthening of the Civil Rights Section. Its proposals included greater appropriations and staff, establishment of field offices, and elevation to the status of a full division in the Department of Justice. Bills have been introduced in Congress to accomplish some or all of these changes.

F. EMERGENCY DETENTION UNDER THE INTERNAL SECURITY ACT OF 1950

This section discusses a civil liberty problem which has not yet arisen.

It will be recalled that during World War II enemy aliens thought to be dangerous were placed in internment camps and that all Japanese-American citizens on the west coast were shut up in "War Relocation Centers." Under executive order which brought about the Japanese-American evacuation, some two hundred individual citizens were required on security grounds to move out of other "defense areas" in which they were living and take up residence elsewhere.

These World War II policies were more or less *ad hoc*, and we do not regard some of them now with much pride and satisfaction. The Internal Security Act of 1950, therefore, seeks to regularize these drastic actions by providing in advance for what is called "emergency detention."

The provisions are briefly these: The President is empowered to proclaim an "internal security emergency" if our territory is invaded, if war is declared by Congress, or if there is an insurrection in the country in aid of a foreign enemy. In such an emergency the President, through the Attorney General, may detain any person "as to whom there is reasonable ground to believe that such person probably will engage in, or probably will conspire with others to engage in, acts of espionage or of sabotage."

Such person is to be confined in a place of detention provided by the Attorney General. Within forty-eight hours after detention he shall be given a hearing before a preliminary hearing officer. At this hearing he is to be told the grounds of his detention, is to be represented by counsel if he so desires, is allowed to introduce evidence in his behalf, and is permitted to cross examine witnesses against him except those whom the Attorney General in the interests of national security does not wish to have appear. From an adverse finding by this preliminary hearing officer, the detainee has the right to appeal to a bipartisan Detention Review Board of nine members, and from their decision either he or the Attorney General, depending on the Board's decision, may appeal to the United States Court of Appeals, which may set aside the order of the Board.

In spite of the elaborate safeguards set up here and the obvious necessity for protecting the national security, there will be sharp controversy over the propriety of interning an American citizen on the basis, not of unlawful conduct, but of what officers of the government believe he will "probably" do. The doctrine of "protective arrests," so familiar a practice in totalitarian countries, has never found favor with us.

SELECTED READINGS

Robert K. Carr, *Federal Protection of Civil Rights* (Ithaca: Cornell University Press, 1947) is an authoritative study of the history and work of the Civil Rights Section in the Department of Justice. See also Francis Biddle, "Civil Rights and Federal Laws," in *Safeguarding Civil Liberty Today* (Ithaca: Cornell University Press, 1945). More general discussions are found in Milton R. Konvitz, *The Constitution and Civil Rights* (New York: Columbia University Press, 1947); Thomas I. Emerson and David Haber, *Political and Civil Rights in the United States,* Chapter I, "The Right to Security of the Person" (Buffalo: Dennis and Company, Inc., 1952).

A notable document, with far-reaching proposals for the protection of civil rights, is *To Secure These Rights: The Report of the President's Committee on Civil Rights* (Washington: Government Printing Office, 1947).

· V ·

Military Power and Civil Liberty

IN TIME of war, in areas where martial law is in force, normal civil liberties are suspended. This occurred in Hawaii during World War II. These problems lie outside the scope of this analysis. So also do the problems connected with military discipline of the armed forces through courts martial. But our civil and military authorities have to live together in times of peace, and civil liberty problems do arise from their normal interaction. The following items suggest some of the forms which these problems may take:

In England and America military power has always been kept subordinate to civil authority. History is replete with convincing reasons for this rule. The issue of military versus civilian control was sharply argued when Congress was debating the Atomic Energy Act of 1946. It was strongly urged that management of our entire atomic energy program should be given to the military branch of the government. The decision of Congress to maintain civilian control was in line with the American tradition. When the National Executive Committee of the American Legion, in

November, 1951, formally resolved that "the management of the Korean War shall be placed in the hands of the military, who shall proceed, considering military problems alone, to a victory," they were probably unaware of the dangerous implications of their proposal.

After the three-day "Operation Alert" in July, 1955, President Eisenhower announced that in the event of an atomic bomb attack he would proclaim martial law throughout the country. While the public, usually not upset by things which have not yet happened, took the proposal calmly, the implications of the proposal aroused deep concern and sharp controversy in groups familiar with these problems.

In 1951 a new Uniform Code of Military Justice was put into effect. In addition to relaxing in some respects the severity of military discipline, it created for the first time a *civilian* Court of Military Appeals to review court martial cases. The new code has aroused controversy. Many army officers feel that discipline has been too seriously weakened by it.

Two problems have arisen affecting the rights of American soldiers in peacetime: The first arose in the Toth case. Toth was honorably discharged from the Air Force in December, 1952. In May, 1953, he was arrested in Pittsburgh for murder allegedly committed in Korea in September, 1952, before his discharge. Toth was flown to Korea by the air force in order to try him by court martial. The case was taken into the federal courts through habeas corpus, and in 1955 the Supreme Court held, six to three, that a former serviceman, like any other civilian, is entitled to all the safeguards afforded those who are tried in the regular federal constitutional courts and may not be subjected to court martial. Since the federal Criminal Code does not provide for the trial of murder or other statutory crimes abroad, Toth could not be tried there, and he was therefore released. (*United States ex rel. Toth* v. *Quarles,* 350 U.S. 11, 1955.)

The second problem relates to American soldiers who commit crimes while stationed abroad. What happens to an American soldier stationed in one of these countries who commits a crime, say burglary or assault, in Paris? The problem was dealt with by Article VII of the NATO Status of Forces Agreement, signed in 1951, effective 1953. The section is summarized by an official of the Department of Justice as follows:

Briefly, the Article provides that each state has exclusive jurisdiction over offenses relating to security which are not violations of the law of the other state. The sending state [United States] also has the primary right to exercise jurisdiction over offenses against its persons and property and over offenses committed in the line of duty. For all other offenses, the receiving state [i.e., Germany, etc.] has primary jurisdiction. It shall, however, give "sympathetic consideration" to a request for a waiver of jurisdiction.

This situation has been blown up into a rather dramatic civil liberty issue, both in Congress and in the press. It has been stated that an American soldier involuntarily ordered abroad may, under this agreement, be tried for a civilian crime in a French court by procedures which may violate the guarantees of our Bill of Rights.

In an exhaustive legal memorandum submitted by the Attorney General to the Senate Foreign Relations Committee in 1953, the following points, among others, were made: First, an American citizen does not carry the protections of the Bill of Rights with him into a foreign country as a matter of constitutional right, a point which the Supreme Court settled in respect to civilians in the Ross case back in 1891. (*In re Ross,* 140 U.S. 453.) Second, international law does not recognize the rights asserted on behalf of American soldiers abroad; this is best shown by the fact that the United States has always claimed and exercised full jurisdiction to try for civilian crime under American law the military personnel of a foreign power stationed in this country. Other countries enjoy the same jurisdiction. Third, it therefore follows that the Status of Forces Agreement gives to our soldiers in NATO countries a more favorable status with respect to possible criminal punishment than they would otherwise have enjoyed.

SELECTED READINGS

A useful discussion of the problems dealt with in this section is Louis Smith, *American Democracy and Military Power* (Chicago: Chicago University Press, 1951). In a symposium edited by Jerome G. Kerwin, *Civil-Military Relationships in American Life* (Chicago: University of Chicago Press, 1948), some of the same topics are discussed.

James R. Newman and Byron Miller, *The Control of Atomic Energy* (New York: McGraw-Hill, 1948), traces the development of our policies in regard to the control of atomic energy, including the controversy over civilian versus military control of the program.

· VI ·

The Civil Liberties of Persons Accused of Crime

THERE is no more accurate index of a nation's regard for civil liberty than is to be found in the laws and procedures by which it deals with persons accused of crime. While, as Justice Frankfurter has observed, "the safeguards of liberty have frequently been forged in controversies involving not very nice people," it is also true that some innocent persons are accused and tried for crime and that even in dealing with guilty persons the self-respect of the community demands that they be treated with justice and fair play.

The basic principles of civil liberty in this important field have long since been embodied in constitutions and statutes and have been fortified by court decisions. The following summary seeks to present the recent issues and controversies which have emerged in the field of criminal justice.

A. SECURING THE EVIDENCE

1. UNREASONABLE SEARCHES AND SEIZURES

The right of the people to be secure in their persons, houses, papers, and effects, against unreasonable searches and seizures, shall not be violated, and no warrants shall issue, but upon probable cause, supported by oath or affirmation, and particularly describing the place to be searched, and the persons or things to be seized.—U.S. CONSTITUTION, FOURTH AMENDMENT

This Amendment forbids the national government to invade the important rights which it describes. Over the years the Supreme Court, in numerous cases, has given concrete meaning to this ban against unreasonable searches and seizures. This it continues to do, and the notable developments with respect to this important liberty since the end of World War II are the following:

a. No clause of the Constitution specifically forbids the states to indulge in unreasonable searches and seizures. In 1949, however, in *Wolf* v. *Colorado* (338 U.S. 25), the Supreme Court declared: "The security of one's privacy against arbitrary intrusion by the police—which is at the core of the Fourth Amendment—is basic to a free society. It is therefore in 'the concept of ordered liberty' and as such enforceable against the states through the Due Process Clause." A possible concrete result of this ruling is that it affords a basis for the federal prosecution under the Civil Rights Act of state or local officers who engage in unreasonable searches and seizures.

b. The Wolf decision was, however, a hollow victory, for the Court in that case reaffirmed its earlier rule that a state may, without denial of due process of law, use in a criminal prosecution evidence which it has secured by unreasonable search and seizure. In short, the states were told not to resort to unreasonable searches, but were still allowed to use the fruits of such searches. As early as 1914, in the Weeks case *(Weeks* v. *United States,* 232 U.S. 383), the

Supreme Court held that evidence secured by unreasonable searches and seizures conducted by *federal* officers could not be used in a *federal* prosecution. Two-thirds of the states allow the use in state courts of such evidence no matter how it is obtained. In the Wolf case the Court refused to make the federal rule apply in the state courts.

c. It had long been held that officers in making a lawful arrest could validly search the person and immediate surroundings of the one arrested. The rule had been fairly strictly construed. In 1947 in *Harris* v. *United States* (331 U.S. 145) the Supreme Court upheld the right of federal officers who had arrested Harris in his home to search his entire five-room apartment. The evidence thus found was used to convict him. Four Justices dissented vigorously against what they regarded as a serious restriction upon the protection against unreasonable searches and seizures.

d. In several cases the Supreme Court had followed the rule that a search was unreasonable if made without a warrant, provided there was adequate time in which to get the warrant. Thus the search without a warrant of a distillery (which, after all, could not get up and walk away) was held to be unreasonable. *(Trupiano* v. *United States,* 334 U.S. 699, 1948.) In the Rabinowitz case in 1950 *(United States* v. *Rabinowitz,* 339 U.S. 56), the Court essentially abandoned this rule which "requires a search warrant solely upon the basis of the practicability of procuring it, rather than upon the reasonableness of the search after lawful arrest." Here again there were strong dissents.

e. In the Olmstead case in 1928 *(Olmstead* v. *United States,* 277 U.S. 438) the Supreme Court held that wiretapping (see below) did not constitute an unreasonable search and seizure within the meaning of the Fourth Amendment because it did not involve a "physical invasion of the premises." It is clear that almost any kind of "mechanical eavesdropping" will be held not to violate the Fourth Amendment. In 1952 in the On Lee case *(On Lee* v. *United States,* 343 U.S. 747) the Supreme Court allowed the use, as evidence validly secured, of the defendant's conversation picked up by a radio transmitter which was concealed in the clothing of a man to whom he was talking and which was listened to and recorded by a witness off the premises. The trend of recent decisions is to give law enforcement agencies the widest possible latitude in the securing of evidence.

There is no adequate analysis of the problems of searches and seizures. Such a study is long overdue.

2. Wiretapping

Wiretapping is a highly controversial topic. The background of the problem is as follows:

In 1928 in the Olmstead case *(supra,* p. 137) the Supreme Court, over strong dissent, held that the tapping of telephone wires in the basement of the building in which a man had his office was not an unreasonable search and seizure and that the evidence thus secured could, therefore, be used against him in federal court. There ensued a flurry of bills in Congress to forbid wiretapping, but none were passed.

In 1934 Congress passed the Federal Communications Act, a section of which forbids any person to intercept any wire messages and to disclose their contents without the sender's consent. In the Nardone case in 1937 *(Nardone* v. *United States,* 302 U.S. 379) the Supreme Court held that this statutory ban on wiretapping applied to federal officers as well as to anyone else and that, since their conduct in wiretapping infringed the statutory rights of those whose wires they tapped, the evidence thus gained could not be used against such persons in a federal court. This did not reverse the Olmstead case. It merely made wiretap evidence inadmissible.

The Department of Justice feels seriously handicapped by the Nardone rule but, by its own construction of the statute, has salvaged some wiretapping powers. The Department's position is that the statute does not forbid the wiretapping, but wiretapping *and* disclosure. Thus the FBI can tap wires, but the government, of course, cannot use this wiretap evidence in court against one whose wires were tapped. But the evidence may be effectively used in other ways. The Nazi saboteurs were caught as a result of evidence secured by a wiretap. The FBI reported to a congressional committee in April, 1955, that it had "fewer" than 150 telephone wires tapped at that time.

This wiretapping by federal agents has its risks, however. Too much zeal may be costly, as was shown in the Judith Coplon case. While the government had a very strong case against Miss Coplon for transmitting government documents to a Russian official, the case was built so completely on wiretap evidence, some of it evidence of conversations between Miss Coplon and her attorney, that it collapsed in court. A new trial was ordered, but the government, one must assume, does not have enough evidence *not* secured by wiretapping to make it worth while to try the case again.

Every Attorney General for twenty years has urged the legalization of the use of wiretap evidence in legal proceedings under certain restrictions. The present Attorney General is backing a bill which would permit designated government agents (chiefly the FBI) to wiretap upon the authorization of the Attorney General in cases involving national security and kidnaping. Evidence so obtained could then, of course, be used in court. Other bills in Congress would permit such wiretaps only upon the authorization of a federal judge. One bill proposed to make the availability of wiretap evidence retroactive so that the government could use the wiretap evidence it has against Miss Coplon and many others. A widespread feeling that this would violate the spirit, if not the letter, of the ex post facto law prohibition, seems likely to prevent the bill from passing.

There is a counterdrive to stiffen the prohibitions against wiretapping. This stems from a widely held conviction that wiretapping is a dishonorable enterprise, a device of totalitarian governments with which our government should not contaminate itself. The uncovering in 1955 of commercialized private wiretapping scandals in New York City, in which private operators sold wiretap evidence for purposes of blackmail, increased the opposition to any relaxation in the law. It is suggested in reply that since we obviously cannot prevent wiretapping no matter how hard we try, we might as well legalize that which will further the ends of law enforcement and the protection of national security and get the benefit of it.

Here is a problem which merits more thorough study than it has received.

3. Self-incrimination

The Fifth Amendment states, "No person...shall be compelled in any criminal case to be a witness against himself." In recent years this has become one of the best-known clauses in the Constitution because of the number of persons who have invoked its protection when asked by legislative investigating committees or other government agencies to testify about previous Communist activities or associations.

a. *Judicial Rules Governing Self-incrimination*

In construing the self-incrimination clause, the courts, over the years, have established the following doctrines:

(1) The protection is not confined to criminal proceedings. It extends to any official inquiry in which testimony under oath may be compelled, such as a coroner's inquest, a grand jury proceeding, or a legislative committee hearing, in which a person is asked questions which might incriminate him.

(2) The protection is against *incrimination*—which means possible prosecution in a court of law. This rule has two results: First, one cannot plead self-incrimination to avoid public humiliation, loss of reputation, or other forms of public disgrace. Second, one cannot plead it if the law cannot possibly reach him, as in the case of one who has been pardoned for a crime or is protected by the statute of limitations.

(3) The protection is a purely personal one. It may not be pleaded in order to avoid testifying against one's relatives, friends, associates, employer, labor union, or any third party or group.

(4) The court has the last word on whether the privilege has been validly pleaded, but in most cases it is bound to rely upon the assertion of the witness that he is entitled to invoke it.

(5) The privilege may be waived, and frequently is. It may also be waived involuntarily by a witness who first

freely testifies in such a way as to incriminate himself and then tries to invoke the privilege. *(Rogers* v. *United States,* 340 U.S. 367, 1951.) When the witness has thus voluntarily incriminated himself he may not refuse to testify further, unless by so doing he would further incriminate himself.

(6) In a federal court the trial judge is required by statute to instruct the jury that the failure of the accused to testify in his own defense does not create any presumption against him. *(Bruno* v. *United States,* 308 U.S. 287, 1939.) Of course, his failure to do so may stem from reasons other than possible self-incrimination. The self-incrimination clause of the Fifth Amendment does not apply to the states, and in some states such unfavorable inferences may be drawn from a defendant's failure to testify. *(Twining* v. *New Jersey,* 211 U.S. 78, 1908.)

(7) The Supreme Court has never had to decide squarely whether or not an innocent man may validly plead self-incrimination. In 1955, however, Chief Justice Warren, quoting from *Twining* v. *New Jersey* (just mentioned), stated that the privilege against self-incrimination is "a protection to the innocent though a shelter to the guilty," and he argued that it must be liberally construed. It is clear that in many cases the possibility of incrimination might arise from a man's testimony even though he be innocent.

b. *Self-incrimination and Investigations of Communism and Subversion*

Under the rule set out in (2) above, one could not validly plead self-incrimination to avoid testifying about Communist membership or affiliations as long as it was not a crime to be a Communist or to engage in Communist activities. In the Blau case in 1950 *(Blau v. United States,* 340 U.S. 159) the Supreme Court held that the criminal provisions of the Smith Act produce a situation in which testifying about one's activity as a Communist Party official created "more than a mere imaginary possibility" of future prosecution. Later, the right to plead self-incrimination was extended to those who were merely members of the Communist Party. *(Brunner v. United States,* 343 U.S. 918, 1952.) Since 1950 some five hundred persons have pleaded the Fifth Amendment when asked to testify before legislative committees or grand juries.

(1) *Reasons for pleading self-incrimination in these cases.* Many different motives have led witnesses to plead self-incrimination when questioned about their possible Communist affiliations. Some fear actual incrimination because of present Communist Party membership or fear various reprisals or stigmas if they admit past membership. Some resent legislative inquiries and their methods and use the plea to obstruct the inquiry, even though they have nothing damaging to conceal. Some resort to the plea in order to avoid giving evidence against their friends. It is clear that some of these reasons for invoking the plea are not legally acceptable, but if the witness is discreet in not announcing his motives, there may be no ground upon which to reject the plea. There is reason to believe that some of these witnesses are not subversives at all, but are rather conscientious objectors with respect to the obligations which the law imposes upon witnesses in these inquiries.

What stands out is the dearth of knowledge about the real reasons why many of these people have invoked the privilege against self-incrimination. A study of this whole complex situation is highly desirable.

(2) *Reprisals upon those who plead self-incrimination.* The man who pleads self-incrimination when asked about his past ties with communism escapes criminal prosecution for past subversive conduct and escapes punishment for contempt of the committee or court which is asking him the questions. He does not, however, escape serious reprisals imposed either legally or unofficially, or both.

The laws of several states (and local governments) require the dismissal of any officer or employee who pleads self-incrimination under lawful inquiry into his past official conduct and, more recently, into his past or present Communist affiliations. The rule has been applied widely to public school teachers. In 1954 President Eisenhower added the self-incrimination plea to the list of items justifying dismissal of a federal employee under the Security Order. In the District of Columbia a secondhand furniture dealer was refused a license to do business because he had pleaded the Fifth Amendment. And Congress, in 1954, forbade payment of any "annuity or retired pay" to any federal officer or employee who pleads self-incrimination before any federal grand jury, court, or congressional committee. These disqualifications assume that persons who plead self-incrimination are unfit to hold positions of public trust.

In April, 1956, the Supreme Court (five to four) held invalid as a denial of due process the New York City charter provision requiring the automatic dismissal of any city employee who pleads self-incrimination when questioned. (*Slochower* v. *Board of Education,* 351 U.S. 000.)

c. *The Immunity Statute of 1954*

One way to make a witness testify is to confer on him legal immunity from prosecution; if he cannot be prosecuted, he cannot claim the protection of the self-incrimination clause. Thus by an immunity statute the government is able to obtain a man's testimony by agreeing not to prosecute him. Such federal immunity statutes are by no means new, but until recently they have been of limited application, and confined chiefly to the legal regulation of business. The resentment and frustration felt both by the Department of Justice and by congressional committees at the mounting number of witnesses who plead self-incrimination when asked about possible subversive activities or associations led Congress in 1954 to pass an immunity statute.

Under this Act immunity may be forced upon a witness called to testify regarding matters affecting the national security. This may be done, however, only upon a two-thirds vote of the full congressional committee, or a vote of either house of Congress (if such house is conducting the inquiry), plus the consent of the federal district judge in the district, which may be given only after the Attorney General is heard on the matter if he so wishes. The new Act was invoked in one or two cases, and its validity challenged. In March, 1956, the Supreme Court held that the statute did not violate the Fifth Amendment, and was valid. (*Ullmann* v. *United States,* 350 U.S. 000, 1956.)

d. *Forced Confessions—"Third-Degree" Methods of Getting Evidence*

An ugly and clearly unlawful method of getting evidence is by resort to so-called "third-degree" methods—in short, police brutality. The extent of this abuse is hard to measure, since those guilty of it naturally conceal it and the victims of it are often persons with criminal records whose charges of mistreatment do not prevail against police denials.

To force a confession from a man by physical violence, or by what some recent cases call "psychological coercion," is not only compulsory self-incrimination but also a denial of due process of law. The courts have been very tough in dealing with cases of this kind. Confessions secured by these methods have been excluded, and judicial disapproval has been strong. The problem has been to secure the evidence of official misconduct.

The efforts of the Civil Rights Section in the Department of Justice to prosecute police officers guilty of brutality have been mentioned *(supra,* p. 124). Unhappily, public opinion in many American communities regards the use of "third-degree" methods by the police with indifference, if not tacit approval.

B. THE ARREST

Well-established rights are possessed by persons arrested on criminal charges. Of these the more important are:

1. A *warrant* is required for a criminal arrest unless the crime is being committed in the presence of the arresting officer, or unless the latter has grounds for believing that the person arrested has recently committed a felony. This protects the citizen from groundless and irresponsible arrest. The arrest of Judith Coplon in New York in 1949 without a warrant led the federal court of appeals in New York to grant her a new trial. *(United States* v. *Coplon,* 185 Fed. 2d 629, 1950.)

2. *Habeas corpus* is available to a person who is arrested. It is granted either for the purpose of testing in court the legality of the arrest or for preventing long delay in the

arraignment and formal charging of the arrested person. Habeas corpus has been discussed *supra*, p. 109.

3. *Bail* is normally granted to persons arrested for crimes which are not punishable by death. Named crimes such as murder, rape, or kidnapping may be nonbailable. While the Eighth Amendment does not guarantee bail, it does forbid the charging of "excessive bail." The problem of bail arose in the cases of some of the Communist leaders convicted under the Smith Act. After the eleven Communists were convicted in 1949, the government asked the Court to deny bail pending appeal of the case, asserting that there were no substantial grounds for the appeal (*Dennis* v. *United States*, 341, U.S. 494, 1951) and the defendants were a threat to the national security if left at large; the request was refused and bail was granted. In another case Communists indicted under the Smith Act were granted bail fixed by the federal district judge at $50,000; the court of appeals ordered this bail reduced. There have been bills in Congress (1955) providing for denial of bail in cases involving certain crimes against the national security.

C. THE ACCUSATION

1. INDICTMENT BY GRAND JURY

No person shall be held to answer for a capital, or otherwise infamous crime, unless on a presentment or indictment of a grand jury, except in cases arising in the land or naval forces, or in the militia, when in actual service in time of war or public danger....—U.S. CONSTITUTION, FIFTH AMENDMENT

THE purpose of grand jury indictment, guaranteed in this clause, is twofold: First, the indictment must result from a sifting of evidence against a person designed to make sure that it is substantial evidence and not a flimsy, malicious, or irresponsible charge of crime. Second, the indictment must spell out with great precision the charges against the accused so that he may prepare his defense. He may not be tried on charges which are not in the indictment. Some of the states, which are not bound by the Fifth Amendment, have substituted indictment by "information" (an accusation prepared by the prosecutor) rather than by grand jury, and the federal government indicts by "information" in the case of misdemeanors.

A few problems have arisen here. In 1954 in the Val Lorwin case the Department of Justice asked the dismissal of Mr. Lorwin's indictment for perjury on the ground that the attorney in charge of the case had grossly misrepresented the facts before the grand jury in order to secure the indictment for what he believed to be political purposes.

In 1953 a federal district judge rebuked a federal grand jury for publicly condemning individuals without indicting them. Such action defeats the purpose of the grand jury, which is to protect persons against unfounded accusations of crime, and it also accuses persons who do not have an opportunity to defend themselves in a court trial.

2. THE RULE AGAINST VAGUENESS

There is an old legal maxim that "where the law is uncertain, there is no law," and it has long been established that definitions of crime must be clear and definite, not vague and fuzzy. Due process of law requires this definiteness, on the theory that a man may not be justly punished under a law so vaguely worded that a reasonable man cannot tell when he is violating it. Some recent censorship laws have failed to meet this test (*supra*, p. 13). In fact, these censorship cases are the most important recent cases in which the issue of certainty in a criminal statute has arisen. It should be added that, in general, the courts have been reluctant to invalidate criminal statutes on this ground unless the defects are very obvious.

An indictment charging a man with crime must be very specific indeed. This basic principle was recently applied in dismissing the key counts in the successive indictments of Owen Lattimore for perjury. The second of these had charged Lattimore with perjury for denying under oath that he had been a "follower of the Communist line" or a "promoter of Communist interests." These phrases, said Judge Youngdahl, were fatally vague since "they had no meaning about which men of ordinary intellect could agree." (*United States* v. *Lattimore,* 112 Fed. Supp. 507, 1953; same, 127 Fed. Supp. 405, 1955.) The court of appeals, 1955, upheld this ruling, and the government thereupon abandoned its case against Lattimore.

D. THE TRIAL

1. TRIAL BY JURY

The trial of all crimes, except in cases of impeachment, shall be by jury....—U.S. CONSTITUTION, ART. III, SEC. 2, CL. 3

In all criminal prosecutions the accused shall enjoy the right to a speedy and public trial, by an impartial jury of the State and district wherein the crime shall have been committed....
—U.S. CONSTITUTION, SIXTH AMENDMENT

By these two clauses of the Constitution trial by jury is embedded in our federal system of criminal justice. Trial by jury means here the English comon law trial by jury—

a jury of twelve persons, a unanimous verdict, and a trial judge who charges the jury with respect to the law. The United States Constitution does not require jury trial in state courts (though most state constitutions do), but merely requires, under the due process clause of the Fourteenth Amendment, an essentially "fair" trial.

Civil liberty problems arise from the present-day operation of the jury system. The more important of these are as follows:

a. *Composition of the Jury*

In cases arising over the past ten years, the Supreme Court has established the doctrine that a jury, when required by the federal Constitution, must be drawn from a cross section of the community. Juries have failed to meet this test when women, in states where they are eligible, have been excluded *(Ballard* v. *United States,* 329 U.S. 187, 1946), and when daily wage earners have been excluded. *(Thiel* v. *Southern Pacific Company,* 328 U.S. 217, 1946.) The rule would apply also if Negroes, Mexicans, or any considerable, identifiable group were to be excluded. This doctrine casts doubt upon the validity of juries drawn from a panel of specially qualified people. The so-called "blue ribbon" jury in New York was upheld, five to four, in the Fay case in 1947 *(Fay* v. *New York,* 332 U.S. 261), but only, it seems from the opinion, because it was not very "blue." In other words, the Court found in that case that such juries were, after all, fairly representative of all sectors of the community.

When the problem of discrimination against Negroes in the matter of jury service first arose, the Supreme Court left the burden of proof of such discrimination on the

Negro who was asserting it—a discrimination which in practice he could never prove. (*Virginia* v. *Rives,* 100 U.S. 313, 1880.) In the second "Scottsboro case" (*Norris* v. *Alabama,* 294 U.S. 587, 1935), the Court held that when over many, many years no Negro had ever served on a jury although plenty of Negroes were qualified to serve, the burden rested on the state or county to show that discrimination had not been practiced—and this the state could not do.

While groups or categories of citizens may not be barred from jury duty, there is no requirement that any or all such groups or categories be actually represented on any particular jury. While a Negro is entitled to a jury from which Negroes have not been excluded because of race, he is not entitled to have Negroes on a particular jury.

b. *An Unbiased Jury*

Perhaps more important than the composition of a jury is its freedom from bias. The traditional procedures for the challenging of prospective jurors are designed to assure this impartiality.

The issue of jury impartiality was raised in the Frazier case *(Frazier* v. *United States,* 335 U.S. 497, 1948), in which the Supreme Court rejected the claim that the jury in a narcotics case was biased because it was composed exclusively of federal employees. In the Morford case in 1950, however *(Morford* v. *United States,* 339 U.S. 258)—a case of contempt of the House Committee on Un-American Activities—the Supreme Court held there was denial of a fair trial since the defendant's counsel was denied the right to question prospective government employee jurors as to the possible influence of the Federal Loyalty Program upon their ability to render a just and impartial verdict.

The basically important problem of the effect of uninhibited press and radio reporting of crimes upon the problem of getting an unbiased jury has been discussed *supra,* p. 9. Community hysteria whipped up by "yellow" press and radio stories of crimes may well make it impossible in many instances to empanel a jury which can keep out of its thinking the prejudices and antagonisms thus aroused.

This important problem deserves careful study and analysis.

c. *A Public Trial*

Experience with Star Chamber proceedings in Britain proved that secret trials were likely to result in the denial of justice to the accused. A trial must therefore be open to the public or to appropriate segments of it. The trial judge has considerable discretion to exclude in order to avoid overcrowding or disorder, or to safeguard public health and morality. The basic right involved is that of the defendant to have friends, family, witnesses, and newspapermen rather than the general public. This problem was mentioned in connection with the problem of the freedom of the press, *supra,* p. 11.

d. *A Speedy Trial*

Delay of justice is an old and persistent problem; and since delay of justice is all too often a denial of justice, it raises serious civil liberty problems. Judges, bar associations, and civic organizations are all concerned with the problem and are seeking solutions, but overcrowded court dockets still remain and result in serious denial of right in many cases.

This problem was highlighted by the action of a federal district judge in March, 1955, setting free John David Provoo, who had been indicted for treason, on the ground that his right to a speedy trial guaranteed by the Sixth Amendment had been denied. He had been tried for treason in 1949 for acts alleged to have been committed in 1942–1945. His conviction was reversed in 1953, and the government was just bringing him to trial again in 1955. In October, 1955, the Supreme Court affirmed the disposition of this case. (*United States* v. *Provoo*, 215 Fed. 2d 531, 1955; affirmed without opinion, 350 U.S. 857, 1955.)

2. The Right to Counsel

The Sixth Amendment guarantees to a defendant in a federal court the right "to have the assistance of counsel for his defense." The provision does not bind state courts, but the due process clause of the Fourteenth Amendment requires that state courts accord the right of counsel in all cases where essential justice demands it.

While the Sixth Amendment intended merely to establish the right of a defendant to have his own lawyer present to aid him and not a lawyer provided by the government, it has come to be generally recognized that counsel must be provided by the courts if a defendant cannot afford counsel of his own. The federal government still does not compensate lawyers appointed by the courts to defend indigent defendants. The widely supported proposal for the creation of "public defenders," comparable in status to prosecuting attorneys, is an attempt to deal with this problem effectively. Some communities have public defenders.

The most important civil liberty problem relating to the right to counsel is that of getting competent counsel to represent unpopular defendants. The long and honorable traditions of the American bar should not make this difficult to do. In 1770 John Adams and Josiah Quincy defended in a Massachusetts court the British officers who were being tried for the Boston Massacre. In 1943 Wendell Willkie defended the Communist Schneiderman in the Supreme Court against the government's attempt to denaturalize him. John W. Davis relates that when John Randolph Tucker was chided by his friends for defending the Chicago anarchists in 1887, Randolph replied, "I do not defend anarchy, I defend the Constitution."

Nevertheless, and in spite of exhortations from judges and bar associations, it is getting increasingly difficult to get lawyers to defend Communists in court. There is growing fear of the contamination of "guilt by association," with all its resulting dangers. It may be noted that one of the reasons given by the Attorney General for listing the National Lawyers Guild as a subversive organization is that its members have so frequently defended Communist clients. Should pending proposals to disbar all Communist lawyers be adopted, the problem of securing counsel to defend Communist clients would become increasingly difficult.

One reason why non-Communist lawyers are reluctant to handle the cases of Communist Party members is that the Party itself is reluctant to allow such "outside" lawyers free rein in the handling of the cases. Non-Communist lawyers are understandably reluctant to act under Party supervision in these matters.

Perhaps the most promising solution of this difficult problem lies in the group action of bar associations which can move more effectively than can the individual lawyer. Bar associations in Cleveland, Toledo, and Milwaukee have provided reassuring evidence that Communist defendants can be effectively represented by able and wholly loyal counsel.

It was one of the many facets of the complicated case of Judith Coplon that the Court of Appeals of the District of Columbia held that, by tapping her telephone conversations with her lawyer, the government had deprived her of the effective right of counsel secured by the Sixth Amendment. *(Coplon v. United States,* 191 Fed. 2d 749, 1951.)

3. Confrontation of Witnesses

The Sixth Amendment also guarantees a federal defendant the right "to be confronted with the witnesses against him." This stemmed from long and ugly experience with trials based on secret evidence. The confrontation rule means that in a criminal trial no evidence (with one or two very limited exceptions) may be admitted against the accused except that of witnesses who actually appear in court. Written evidence in the form of depositions is barred. One of the exceptions is the written statement of a dying person, presumed under the circumstances to be truthful. When Judith Coplon was tried in the District of Columbia the government made every effort to avoid the full disclosure of the FBI reports comprising much of the evidence against her. The trial judge ruled that these reports must be made part of the record of the trial or else the government must give up its prosecution.

Confrontation includes the right to cross-examine witnesses. In most criminal trials the question which the jury must decide is which witnesses are to be believed. To answer this question with any hope of correctness the jury must see the witnesses and hear them questioned, so that its members may form their own opinions as to their credibility.

The constitutional right of confrontation of witnesses

exists in criminal prosecutions, and a similar statutory right exists in many administrative proceedings. The right seems so essential to basic justice and fair play that one would suppose that it would be applied in all cases in which charges of misconduct are brought against individuals and are being weighed. This, however, is not the case. The right of confrontation in proceedings before legislative investigating committees, or before loyalty or security boards, is almost invariably denied. This will be further considered *infra,* p. 192.

4. Essential Fairness Required by Due Process of Law

While most of the common law guarantees of fair criminal procedure found in the Bill of Rights do not apply to the state, the states, nevertheless, do not escape the mandate to provide essential "fairness" of procedure which is imposed on them by the due process clause of the Fourteenth Amendment. All the elements that go to make up this fair procedure cannot be fully set out here. Mainly, however, due process prevents the knowing use of perjured testimony and the use of confessions secured through police brutality. And in a notable case many years ago *(Moore* v. *Dempsey,* 261 U.S. 86, 1923) the Supreme Court held that a trial conducted in an atmosphere of mob violence denied due process of law even though all the proper rules of procedure had been observed.

The Court has also held that due process is denied when a defendant is tried for crime before a judge who profits (by the amount of court costs) by the conviction, but not by the acquittal of the accused. *(Tumey* v. *Ohio,* 273 U.S. 510, 1927.)

E. CRUEL AND UNUSUAL PUNISHMENTS

Excessive bail shall not be required, nor excessive fines imposed, nor cruel and unusual punishments inflicted.—U.S. CONSTITUTION, EIGHTH AMENDMENT

No serious current civil liberty problem exists with respect to cruel or inhuman penalties for crime. The history of capital punishment in this country shows that great ingenuity has been directed toward finding less cruel and brutal methods of putting a man to death, rather than the reverse. The Resweber case, in 1947 *(Louisiana* ex rel. *Francis* v. *Resweber,* 329 U.S. 459), raised the issue of cruel punishment in a bizarre way. A Negro boy was to be electrocuted. The electric chair did not work when the execution was attempted. In a five-to-four decision the Supreme Court held that a second attempt at electrocution would not be a cruel and unusual punishment and would not, therefore, be a denial of due process of law. The prisoner was electrocuted. The Court stated that the states are forbidden by the due process clause from inflicting cruel and unusual punishments.

Within limits set by statutes, trial judges usually have wide discretion in imposing fines and prison sentences. There is no clear test of what is excessive in the matter of penalties. In the federal judicial system the appellate courts have no power to change a sentence imposed by the trial judge, though in extreme cases a new trial could be ordered. There is serious discussion at present of a proposal to allow federal courts of appeal to modify sentences that seem excessive.

Penalties for crimes of subversion have always been heavy, and we have recently increased the number of such crimes that are punishable by death. The practice has cropped up here and there, however, of punishing Communists or subversives more heavily than other people for offenses that have nothing to do with subversion, and this is hard to defend. The press reported recently the case of a man brought before a state judge charged with two traffic offenses of a rather common variety. When the judge learned that the defendant was a Communist, he sentenced him to six months in jail for each offense, and made the sentences run consecutively rather than (as is usually done) concurrently.

F. DOUBLE JEOPARDY

... nor shall any person be subject for the same offense to be put twice in jeopardy of life or limb...—U.S. CONSTITUTION, FIFTH AMENDMENT

This provision forbids the federal government to try a man twice for the same offense, unless he himself, upon being convicted, seeks a new trial by an appeal. The government may not appeal a case in which a man has been acquitted, even though serious errors of law occurred in the trial or even though the government may have secured new evidence not previously available. A man is not put in jeopardy until his trial begins. He is not put in jeopardy by being indicted for crime; and therefore the government may indict a man over and over again without violating the jeopardy rule, although it ordinarily does not do so.

There has long been criticism, on civil liberty grounds, of the rule established by the Supreme Court many years ago *(Moore* v. *Illinois,* 14 Howard 13, 1852) that a man is protected against double jeopardy only in the courts of the same government (federal or state) which tried him in the first place. A single act may be a crime against both a state and the United States. In such a case both governments may try the man who commits it without violating the guarantee against double jeopardy. This occurred (*United States* v. *Lanza,* 260 U.S. 377, 1922) in the Prohibition era; Lanza was convicted in both state and federal courts for selling the same case of bootleg whisky. In present practice, trial by both governments almost never occurs; it is prevented by the comity which widely prevails between federal and state law enforcement agencies.

There have been cases in which a man has been tried several times in a federal court for what appears to be the same crime, but under circumstances which did not spell out technical double jeopardy. This has happened to some conscientious objectors, as mentioned *supra,* p. 98. The question is being discussed whether the eleven Communist leaders, now that they have served their prison terms, may *again* be prosecuted for conspiracy to overthrow the government, and so on indefinitely. These cases raise questions as to whether such repeated prosecutions are for fresh crimes, or are in reality for the same crimes. The test would be whether the government could produce evidence of fresh activity upon the part of these people.

G. EX POST FACTO LAWS AND BILLS OF ATTAINDER

No bill of attainder or ex post facto law shall be passed.—U.S. CONSTITUTION, ART. I, SEC. 9, CL. 3

No State shall...pass any bill of attainder, ex post facto law... —U.S. CONSTITUTION, ART. I, SEC. 10, CL. 1

The framers of the Constitution felt that these two guarantees were important enough to be placed in the Constitution itself and to be applicable to both states and federal governments.

1. EX POST FACTO LAWS

While there is some historical evidence that the framers of the Constitution intended by the ex post facto clauses to forbid *all* retroactive legislation, the Supreme Court in an early decision *(Calder v. Bull,* 3 Dallas, 386, 1798) restricted the application of the clause to criminal statutes.

To be ex post facto, a law must meet three tests: first, it must be retroactive; second, it must relate to criminal (and not civil) action; third, it must work to the disadvantage of accused persons (as a class). Retroactive laws which "mitigate the rigor of the law" are not ex post facto.

The civil liberty issues which arise in connection with the ex post facto clauses turn mainly on the question whether a particular retroactive statute is or is not a criminal statute. If it is a criminal statute, it is invalid; if it is not a criminal statute, it is valid. This issue was involved in the Hawker case *(Hawker v. New York,* 170 U.S. 189, 1898), which still remains a controversial case. New York passed a statute forbidding anyone to practice medicine in the state who had ever been convicted of a felony. Hawker, who had served a term in prison for performing an abortion but who had resumed his practice of medicine after his release, found himself deprived of his license. His contention that the statute was ex post facto, since it imposed additional punishment upon him for an earlier crime, had much plausibility and was strongly supported in the dissenting opinions. The Supreme Court held, however, that the New York statute was civil, not criminal. Its purpose was to raise the standards of the medical profession, and not to inflict punishment. In short, a statute is not a criminal statute simply because it inflicts disabilities and losses upon those to whom it applies.

The rule in the Hawker case clearly covers most of the recent legislation declaring persons unfit to hold public office who have in the past engaged in subversive activities or knowingly belonged to subversive organizations. It is generally accepted that these statutes are not penal in character, but merely establish new standards of fitness for public employees.

The proceedings by which the federal government normally deals with aliens are *civil* proceedings: admission to the country, naturalization, denaturalization, and deportation. This means that the ex post facto clause does not prevent Congress from denying any of the privileges involved on the ground of misconduct or questionable associations which lie in the distant past. To deport a man in 1955 because of Communist associations in 1930 is in reality though not in law to inflict severe punishment upon him; but the statute which authorizes this is not ex post facto, because deportation is a civil and not a criminal proceeding.

No civil liberty issue is posed by state habitual-criminal statutes. These laws punish criminals more severely for third or fourth offenses than for a first offense, although the crimes may be similar. New York imposes life imprisonment upon fourth-offender felons. The question is whether the heavy later penalty does not reach back and add fresh punishments for the earlier crimes. Without exception the courts have held that these laws are not ex post facto.

2. BILLS OF ATTAINDER

Bills of attainder are legislative acts which in themselves convict persons of crime and impose punishments upon them. They are closely related to ex post facto laws. Most bills of attainder are likely to be ex post facto definitions of new crimes.

There have been few bills of attainder in our history. At the close of the Civil War, Congress passed a law barring from practice in the federal courts any lawyer who could not swear that he had not aided the Confederate cause. A. H. Garland, who had been an officer in the Confederate government (and who later became Attorney General of the United States), was thus disbarred. The Supreme Court held (*Ex parte* Garland, 4 Wall. 333, 1867) that the statute in question was both a bill of attainder and an ex post facto law. Similar though more drastic provisions set up in Missouri were held invalid on the same grounds *(Cummings* v. *Missouri,* 4 Wall. 277, 1867).

In 1943 Congress attached as a rider to an appropriation act a provision which forbade the payment from the Treasury of money for the salaries of three men, Messrs. Lovett, Watson, and Dodd, who had been found by a committee of the House of Representatives to be disloyal. The men were named in the statute, and their dismissal was to be effected by the stoppage of salary payments. The Supreme Court held the rider to be a bill of attainder. *(United States v. Lovett,* 328 U.S. 303, 1946.) It declared that in the circumstances of the case the dismissal of the three men on grounds of disloyalty amounted to legislative punishment for misconduct.

The Court used language in this case which was fairly broad, with the result that it was widely urged that if a person dismissed from a federal job on grounds of disloyalty was being *punished* (as the Court had said) then he was entitled to the usual protections accorded by the Constitution to persons being tried for crime. These arguments have not prevailed, and the courts have shown no disposition in dealing with problems relating to communism and subversion to apply the bill of attainder prohibition. There has been no case since the Lovett case in which the dismissal of any public employee has been held to be a bill of attainder.

H. TREASON

Treason against the United States, shall consist only in levying war against them, or in adhering to their enemies, giving them aid and comfort. No person shall be convicted of treason unless on the testimony of two witnesses to the same overt act, or on confession in open court.—U.S. CONSTITUTION, ART. III, SEC. 3, CL. 1

This is the only crime defined in the Constitution. These carefully chosen words were intended to prevent prosecutions for the English crime of "constructive" treason, which comprised subversive speeches, propaganda, or other conduct directed against the government.

The treason clause has not been interpreted in this restrictive way, and today we have on the statute books a whole arsenal of legislation punishing a wide range of subversive acts which fall just short of being actual treason. We do not have to prove a man guilty of treason or else let him go free. We can prosecute him for a substantial list of subversive acts which are not labeled "treason" and to which the rigid restrictions of the treason clause do not apply.

It has been mentioned before (*supra*, p. 3) that most of the treason cases which grew out of World War II were cases in which the defendants had engaged in radio broadcasting for the enemy.

SELECTED READINGS

Brief comments on the topics covered in this section are found in some of the general books on civil liberties. Among these are Osmund Fraenkel, *Our Civil Liberties* (New York: Viking Press, 1944); Alison Reppy, *Civil Rights in the United States* (New York: Central Book Company, 1951). More detailed treatment is found in Thomas I. Emerson and David Haber, *Political and Civil Rights in the United States,* Chapter II, "Fairness in Governmental Procedures" (Buffalo: Dennis and Company, Inc., 1952). The entire context in which many of these civil liberties belong is presented in Lester R. Orfield, *Criminal Procedure from Arrest to Appeal* (New York: New York University Press, 1947).

There are monographs on some, but not all, of the provisions in the Bill of Rights discussed in this section. Among these are: Virginia Wood, *Due Process of Law* (Baton Rouge: Louisiana State University Press, 1951); Francis Heller, *The Sixth Amendment to the Constitution of the United States* (Lawrence: University of Kansas Press, 1951); William M. Beaney, *The Right* to *Counsel in American Courts* (Ann Arbor: University of Michigan Press, 1955). On the controversial self-incrimination clause of the Fifth Amendment, see Erwin N. Griswold, *The Fifth Amendment Today* (Cambridge: Harvard University Press, 1955); a more technical discussion presenting a different viewpoint is C. Dickerman Williams, "Problems of the Fifth Amendment," *Fordham Law Review*, XXIV (1955), 19 ff.

The most useful material on these topics is to be found in articles in professional journals. These are often inaccessible to the ordinary reader, but they can be readily traced through the *Index to Legal Periodicals*, found in any good law library.

The Constitution of the United States of America: Analysis and Interpretation (Washington: Government Printing Office, 1953), edited by Edward S. Corwin, contains invaluable annotations on the topics included in this section, as well as on all other provisions of the Constitution.

· VII ·

Civil Liberties and National Security

THE civil liberty issues raised by our security problems are more acute, numerous, and varied than in any other area and of course cut across the normal lines of classification upon which the present conspectus has been built. The reasons for this are not hard to find. The cold war has brought an acute sense of danger to national security. The Communist threat, that of Soviet aggression abroad and of Communist subversion at home, has been frightening. Both justify restraints on liberty which would otherwise be indefensible. We live therefore in a context of balancing safety against freedom, and there is constant dispute over where the lines between the two shall be drawn.

The summary which follows undertakes to do two things: First, it reminds the reader of the nature and variety of the methods we are currently using in our program for national security; second, it lists the major threats to civil liberty which have emerged in the operation of this program.

A. SCOPE AND NATURE OF OUR PROGRAM TO PROTECT OUR NATIONAL SECURITY

Briefly, the statutes, executive orders, court decisions, policies, and practices which comprise our present arsenal against communism and subversion deal with the following subjects:

1. COUNTERESPIONAGE

One of the most obvious and effective ways to deal with espionage and similar threats to national security is by counterespionage. We are well equipped with agencies to carry on such work. Most important are the FBI and the Central Intelligence Agency, although professional investigating units exist in half a dozen other departments of the government.

2. LAWS TO PROTECT THE NATION'S SECRETS

Congress has passed various laws to insure the protection of national secrets. The Espionage Act of 1917 punishes the giving of information to the enemy or to a foreign country, and it will be recalled that the Rosenbergs were convicted under this statute. Other statutes less well known forbid the similar transmission of government documents or like information. The Atomic Energy Act of 1946 forbids the disclosure of information regarding atomic weapons.

These statutes are supplemented, of course, by numerous executive and military regulations designed to ensure secrecy. Perhaps the most notable is President Eisenhower's Executive Order 10501 issued in 1953, which sets up rules for the classifying and handling of government secrets throughout the executive branch. This order established the three categories, "top secret," "secret," "confidential."

3. Laws to Prevent Alien Subversion

The civil liberties of aliens are dealt with later (p. 208). Not only are aliens peculiarly subject to governmental restraints because of their lack of many constitutional rights, but they have been viewed as posing uniquely dangerous threats to our internal security. The government's efforts to meet these threats will be found in the four types of legislation under which we deal with aliens generally:

a. *Immigration*

While we provided for the deportation of undesirable aliens as far back as 1798, our policy of excluding aliens believed to be dangerous dates from 1903, when we began barring anarchists. The Internal Security Act of 1950 added Communists and other totalitarians to the excluded group. The Immigration and Nationality Act of 1952 (Walter-McCarren Act) contained much more elaborate and more drastic provisions; one of these bars any alien, if any consular official or the Attorney General knows or has reasonable grounds to believe that he will engage in activities contrary to the public security.

The registration and fingerprinting of aliens was required by Congress in 1940 (The Smith Act). The Act of 1952 elaborates this and creates a central file of all aliens in the United States.

b. *Naturalization*

The Act of 1952 bars from naturalization Communists, members of Communist or Communist-front organizations, and all persons who teach, advocate, or publish the Communist doctrine of the violent overthrow of government. The ban is retroactive on those who within ten years of the application for naturalization have belonged in one of these classes.

c. *Denaturalization*

The Act of 1952 spells out new grounds for denaturalization. Among these are: concealing at the time of naturalization membership in a subversive organization; refusing within ten years following naturalization to testify before a congressional committee with regard to subversive activities if the person has been convicted of contempt because of such refusal; becoming within five years after naturalization a member of an organization if such membership in the first place would have prevented naturalization. This creates a prima facie case for denaturalization.

d. *Deportation*

The Act of 1952 adds a most controversial retroactive provision. This provision permits the deportation of any alien who is, or who at any time after his entry into the country *has been* a member of the various organizations designated as subversive. This makes mandatory the deportation of an alien who at any time after his entry was a Communist even though he may long since have left the Party. The statute allows the Attorney General in certain limited cases to suspend deportation, and Congress very occasionally intervenes by special act for the same purpose.

4. Loyalty and Security Programs

These programs are designed to prevent the employment, either in the government or in other strategic areas of employment, of persons who either are disloyal or are security risks. It is estimated that some ten million persons are now subject to these screening programs. The security-loyalty programs deal with the following groups of employees:

a. *Federal Employees*

The Hatch Act of 1939 forbade the employment by the government of persons committed to the overthrow of the government by force and violence. Appropriation bills beginning with that of 1941 have all similarly forbidden such employment. In 1943 President Roosevelt created an Interdepartmental Committee on Employee Loyalty. With the aid of the FBI this committee was to review a docket of loyalty cases, explore the loyalty problem generally, and make recommendations.

In 1947 President Truman, by executive order, established the first federal loyalty program. Among other things this ordered the compiling of the Attorney General's list of subversive organizations. When first announced, the program called for denying federal employment when "on all the evidence, reasonable grounds exist for the belief that the person involved is disloyal to the government of the United States." In 1951 the President changed this order so that it barred persons about whose loyalty there was "reasonable doubt."

In 1953 President Eisenhower, by executive order, established his security program. This was originally intended to distinguish between (1) disloyal employees and (2) loyal employees who were nevertheless security risks. The difficulties inherent in making this distinction are commented on later (*infra,* p. 183). The new program sets up as the basic test of employee fitness a finding that "the retention in employment in the federal service of the person being investigated is clearly consistent with the interests of national security." In the administration of this program, boards and security officers are not limited to the use of the Attorney General's list.

There are other federal security programs. The armed services operate several, and another covers marine and water-front employees.

In 1953 the President, by executive order, set up a loyalty-security program for United States citizens employed by the United Nations. The findings reached under this program, however, are advisory only.

b. *State Employees*

The states as a rule have not established elaborate security-loyalty programs, after the federal pattern, for the screening of state employees. An exception to this may be noted in the case of public school teachers in many areas, although even here permanent loyalty-security machinery does not exist in most states. In 1951 New York passed the Security Risk Law, which authorizes the Civil Service Commission to screen for loyalty and security all applicants for state jobs.

The states proceed in other ways. In some states members of the Communist Party are kept off the election ballot by law. In some states public officers and employees are screened by requiring them to take a loyalty oath; the Ober law in Maryland illustrates this method.

c. *Private Industry under Defense Contracts*

Part of the government's defense work is done under contract by private industry, and this includes highly secret enterprises. As a result, security screening is required by executive order of those employed by private industry in the carrying on of classified projects or contracts. There is a tendency to enlarge the scope of this security clearance. Senator Butler (Maryland) has introduced a bill which would extend it to all employees of any plant having any defense contracts. It should be added that security programs are in some cases operated by private industries on their own initiative, either in anticipation of defense contracts or on general principles.

d. *Labor Unions*

The provision for loyalty oaths in the Taft-Hartley Act of 1947 has been discussed (*supra,* p. 50). The Communist Control Act of 1954 has provisions for identifying "Communist-infiltrated organizations," and if a labor union is found to be infiltrated it forfeits its privileges of collective bargaining.

5. Loyalty Oaths

No important civil liberty problems are posed by the type of loyalty oath which requires merely the swearing of support to the Constitution or some similar expression of present loyalty to the government.

Loyalty oaths of the old "test oath" variety are not at all the same. They require sworn statements as to past and present loyalty and impose various disabilities upon those who cannot or will not take the oath. Requirements of this sort have spread with great rapidity during the past few years.

a. *Federal Requirements for Loyalty Oaths*

Congress has not required any blanket loyalty oath as part of its program against communism and subversion.

The loyalty and security programs have no doubt made this seem unnecessary.

One or two exceptions may be noted. The so-called Gwinn Amendment, in 1952, to the federal housing legislation bars from federal housing units any person who is a member of any organization designated as subversive by the Attorney General. This is on the theory, as Congressman Gwinn expressed it, that "public housing breeds Communism." In enforcing this provision, housing authorities have required prospective tenants to swear that they were not members of any of the proscribed organizations. The constitutionality of the Gwinn Amendment was promptly challenged. One or two lower courts held it unconstitutional, and the Court of Appeals in the District of Columbia held that a tenant could not be validly barred because of his refusal to take the required oath, since his failure to do so did not prove membership in any forbidden organization. *(Rudder v. United States,* 226 Fed. 2d 51, 1955.) The Supreme Court of Wisconsin held the Gwinn Amendment unconstitutional, and the Supreme Court of the United States denied certiorari. *(Lawson v. Housing Authority,* 70 N.W. 2d 605; 350 U.S. 135, 1955.) In all probability the Supreme Court will have to decide whether the Gwinn Amendment is valid.

In 1953 the armed services required a very elaborate loyalty oath from applicants for commissions in the ROTC. This was a comprehensive "test oath" relating to the student officer's entire past record. Protests against this led the Department of Defense in 1955 to substitute for it a simple oath declaring present loyalty to the government.

In 1955 Senator Eastland introduced a bill which would require a loyalty oath of any attorney appearing before any federal court or agency.

b. *State Requirements for Loyalty Oaths*

The "test" type of loyalty oath has spread rapidly throughout the states. Teachers' oaths were discussed above. (*Supra,* p. 80.)

State oaths differ in form from each other, though in general they tend to require a sworn disavowal of present and past Communist membership and membership in designated organizations. Five years of past loyalty is a time period commonly required. Many of these state and local loyalty oaths accept membership in an organization on the Attorney General's list as conclusive evidence of unfitness for public employment, although the President's loyalty order creating the list does not do so, and federal courts have held that such membership cannot be made conclusive evidence of disloyalty. (*Schachtman* v. *Dulles,* 225 Fed. 2d 938, 1955.)

A complete list of all the persons from whom loyalty oaths are required would be very long. Some of these are: public employees including school teachers; authors and publishers of school textbooks (Texas); persons holding insurance licenses (the District of Columbia); public accountants (New York); persons eligible for unemployment compensation (Ohio); wrestlers and prize fighters (Indiana); students in state universities (Texas). Particularly controversial is the California 1952 oath requirement imposed on persons and organizations enjoying tax exemptions; it therefore applies to all churches and has been sharply attacked.

6. Crimes against National Security, Federal and State

a. *Crimes of Action*

We have adequate laws against treason, sabotage, espionage, and various activities directed against our military establishments or our secrecy restrictions.

b. *Crimes of Advocacy*

Federal statutes of this variety are the Espionage Act of 1917 and the Smith Act of 1940. Practically every state has some kind of legislation against sedition, and laws on antisyndicalism. See the comment on the free speech implications of these laws (*supra,* p. 3). In 1954 the Supreme Court of Pennsylvania held invalid a Pennsylvania statute making it a state crime to advocate the overthrow of government by force and violence, on the ground that the Smith Act completely occupied the field and rendered competing laws invalid. (*Pennsylvania* v. *Nelson,* 377 Pa. 58.) In April, 1956, the Supreme Court of the United States affirmed this decision and thereby invalidated the sedition laws of some forty states. (*Pennsylvania* v. *Nelson,* 350 U.S. 000, 1956.)

7. Disclosure Requirements for Subversives or Potential Subversives

a. *The Foreign Agents' Registration Act of 1938*

Amended in 1953, this Act requires the agents of any "foreign principal" to register with the Department of Justice, to file statements about their activities and affairs, and to label any "political propaganda" they circulate.

b. *The Alien Registration Act of 1940*

Supplemented by the Immigration and Nationality Act of 1952, the Act requires all resident aliens in this country to be "registered" and fingerprinted and requires comprehensive information about them.

c. *The Internal Security Act of 1950*

This Act requires the registration of "Communist action" or "Communist-front" organizations. The procedures for accomplishing this are very elaborate, and no such organization has up to now been registered. None has done so voluntarily, and the validity of the statute is now before the Supreme Court. (*Communist Party of United States* v. *Subversive Activities Control Board*, 351 U.S. 000, 1956.)

d. *The Communist Control Act of 1954*

By this Act, "Communist-infiltrated" organizations were added to the two groups required to register under the Act of 1950.

8. Disabilities and Loss of Privileges Imposed on Subversives

The most obvious disability imposed by the federal government is of course loss of one's job. Another disability is the loss of the privilege to travel either into or out of the country, a loss effected by federal regulations with respect to immigration, deportation, passports, and visas. Mention has been made (p. 173) of the statute attempting to bar subversives from federal housing units. As a result of the Alger Hiss case, Congress has cut off federal pensions to those convicted of crimes of subversion.

The many disabilities imposed upon subversives by state and local laws are usually imposed through loyalty oath requirements. These have been discussed (*supra,* p. 174).

9. Legislative Committees Investigating Subversion

Committees of Congress and of several state legislatures have been active in the effort to uncover Communist and subversive activities. Some phases of this committee activity are dealt with *infra,* p. 194.

10. Private Activities Directed Against Communism and Subversion

These private activities vary widely not only in kind but in the degree of responsibility with which they are carried on. They are discussed *infra,* p. 201.

B. DEVIATIONS FROM TRADITIONAL CIVIL LIBERTY PRINCIPLES

To study the impact on civil liberties of each item in our elaborate program against subversion is impossible here. Exhaustive studies of major parts of the security program are going forward. Studies of the legislative committees dealing with subversion are already available.

What is attempted here is to single out the established civil liberty principles which are thought to have been either violated or seriously threatened by the subversive-control program. And it should be made clear that what is being discussed is not the enforcement of criminal statutes against treason or other forms of subversion. Persons duly charged with these crimes enjoy, as a matter of course, the constitutional rights already discussed, *supra,* Ch.VI.

A prudent goverment is duty bound to rid itself of those who would undermine its institutions and jeopardize its safety or who cannot fairly be trusted to hold public office or employment. This is a serious responsibility.

But in a democratic state it is necessary to be sure that this vitally important job is being done by the right people, by the right methods, according to the right standards, and for the right motives. A free government cannot smugly operate on the principle that the end justifies the means. It must constantly scrutinize the means to be sure that the costs of internal security, in terms of sacrifice of individual rights and freedoms, are not excessive.

The civil liberty issues generated by the program stem in large part from the fact that what the program tries to do is to *identify* those who are Communists, subversive, or disloyal, as well as those who are "security risks" by reason of doubt as to their loyalty or reliability. A wide range of governmental agencies—federal, state, and local, plus various private groups—have felt impelled to "get into the act" and help expose these undesirable or dubious characters. Public opinion, frightened by the cold war and the danger of internal treachery, has approved of having as many Communist hunters as possible.

In the process of "exposure" of disloyal or suspect persons a number of genuinely disloyal persons have been brought to light and have been convicted of crime. Others have been shown to be of dubious loyalty and have been properly barred from posts of public trust. Others have been accused irresponsibly, or on unreliable evidence, of disloyal or subversive affiliations, and these persons have suffered in many cases almost as much as those who were actually disloyal. To be "exposed" is to be branded—and in most cases indelibly so—and the brand results not from the guilt but from the exposure.

What this adds up to is that this process of "exposure," necessary as it is, inevitably results in punishment of the persons exposed.

Such punishment is not known to the criminal law, but it is not less real on that account. In many cases it may be more lasting and devastating than fine or imprisonment. The Supreme Court recognized this in referring to one phase of the program. It said, "There can be no dispute about the consequences visited upon a person excluded from public employment on disloyalty grounds. In the view of the community the stain is a deep one; indeed it has become a badge of infamy." *(Wieman v. Updegraff,* 344 U.S. 183, 1952.) And Walter Lippmann, commenting on "exposure" by congressional committees, has said, "As exercised by latter-day congressional committees, the power to investigate is a tremendous instrument, combining the power to make laws, to enforce those laws, to judge and to punish men under those laws. This tremendous instrument can be, notoriously it has been, used to harass, to intimidate, to punish, and to destroy."

Thus the "exposure" of Communists, subversives, security risks, and anyone suspected of being any of these, has become in the present climate of opinion a punishment in fact, if not in law. This seems to be true whether the result is intended or not. If we resort to exposure then we assume an obligation to make sure that in punishing people by "exposure" we conform as rigidly as possible to the basic principles and procedures which the American tradition of civil liberty and fair play extend to those who are "punished."

The following analysis attempts to indicate some of the ways in which, in our complex and multifarious campaign against communism and subversion, we have tended to deviate from long-established traditions of civil liberty. The purpose is not to prove that we should no longer attempt to protect our internal security, but rather to suggest that these deviations from the American tradition are not in fact necessary to our national safety. The more important of these deviations are discussed below.

1. THE DOCTRINE OF SEPARATION OF POWERS

The American constitutional system is built on the doctrine of the separation of the powers of government. One could quote at length from our early statesmen to show their conviction that this separation of powers was essential if governmental tyranny was to be prevented. Such tyranny would almost inevitably ensue if legislative, executive, and judicial powers rested in the same hands. Peculiar danger to the rights of citizens would result if legislative or executive officers were to exercise judicial power. In 1926 Justice Brandeis, dissenting in *Myers* v. *United States* (272 U.S. 52), observed, "The doctrine of the separation of powers was adopted by the Convention of 1787, not to promote efficiency but to preclude the exercise of arbitrary powers." It may be added that Representative Martin Dies, while chairman of the House Committee on Un-American Activities, listed, as one of the badges of un-Americanism, a man's failure to believe in our system of checks and balances and in our system of separation of governmental powers.

Earlier in the history of the Dies Committee its chairman stated bluntly that its most important and valuable function would be the "exposure" of persons who were disloyal or un-American. Subsequent committees investigating subversion have proceeded on this principle and have tended to regard inquiries aimed at the proposal of legislation (the normal function of such a committee) as subsidiary to this task of "exposure."

We need not labor the point that this exposure is in effect punishment of the persons exposed, and committee members have been frank in saying that this is intentional and desirable.

In January, 1956, the Court of Appeals in the District of Columbia held, two to one, that a congressional committee is without constitutional power to question a witness for the purpose of exposure of persons "to public contempt or hostility." The questions served no valid legislative purpose. (*Watkins* v. *United States*, 000 Fed. 2d 000.) The full Court of Appeals of the District, a court of nine judges, has reheard but not yet decided the case. The case will almost certainly be carried to the Supreme Court. But even if the Supreme Court holds that "exposure" is a valid purpose for a congressional committee to pursue, the individual citizen who suffers punishment inflicted by such "exposure" is the victim of a violation of the spirit of the basic doctrine that judicial power (to punish) may not be exercised by the legislature.

2. Definiteness of Loyalty and Security Standards

In the discussion of criminal justice (*supra,* p. 148), it was pointed out that one of the fundamental rights guaranteed by due process of law is the right to have criminal statutes define clearly and definitely those acts which are declared to be crimes. Essential justice requires that a person not be punished for committing an offense so vaguely defined that a reasonable man could commit the crime without knowing it. A long line of Supreme Court decisions establish this rule.

It is clear that in determining whether a person is a Communist, a subversive, or a disloyal person there should be definitions or criteria by which to decide whether he falls into one of these groups. If Congress or any state legislature were to make disloyalty a crime, it would be obliged to define disloyalty with such precision that it would meet the basic test of certainty under due process of law.

The history of the efforts of our legislative and administrative agencies to define subversion and disloyalty reveals vagueness and confusion in the standards by which persons are judged to be subversive or disloyal.

The story begins with the efforts of the Dies Committee followed by one of two state legislative committees to track down and expose "un-Americanism." It is obvious that the word "un-American" has no legal meaning and can have none. This word is charged with emotional feeling, and what it means depends upon what is in the mind of the one who uses it. The Dies Committee recognized this and was a bit embarrassed by it as shown by the series of committee reports in which the term "un-Americanism" was variously explained. Here perhaps belongs the classic remark of Mr. J. Parnell Thomas, a member of that Committee, that "anyone who opposes the work of this Committee is un-American."

a. *Truman Loyalty Order of 1947*

When the Truman loyalty program was set up in 1947 for the express purpose of barring from federal employment persons who were disloyal, it was clearly necessary to define, if possible, what "disloyalty" means. The order did not attempt to define "loyalty," but only "disloyalty." A clear and precise definition was obviously impossible, since here, as in the case of the term "un-American," the meaning of "disloyalty" is determined in large part by subjective rather than objective tests. An effort was made, however, to guide loyalty boards in making determinations of disloyalty, and the order made a list of types of behavior which might lead to a conclusion that an employee was disloyal. Here were listed a number of items not open to debate, such as acts of treason, sabotage, espionage, and other crimes against national security. Much less definite was the test of "sympathetic affiliation" with any organization designated by the Attorney General as Communist, Fascist, or subversive.

What stands out here is the fact that a man could be branded as disloyal to the United States and deprived of his job for conduct, associations, or utterances so vaguely described (or not described at all) that he could not possibly have foreseen that they would constitute disloyalty. Nor did the order give him a clearer picture of what would be held to constitute disloyalty in the future.

The standards by which persons were dismissed from the federal service under the loyalty program were sharply criticized. It was felt that they lacked sharpness of definition and that, as applied, in many cases they had resulted in injustice. Furthermore, they provided no answer to the problem of "security risks" who were admittedly loyal. All disloyal persons are security risks, but not all security risks are disloyal, as, for example, alcoholics or persons notoriously indiscreet. The Eisenhower Security Program of 1953 was designed at the outset to draw this distinction and to avoid the injustice arising from confusing security risks with disloyal persons.

b. *Eisenhower Security Order of 1953*

The Security Program of 1953 retained the disloyalty tests in the Truman program and added an additional list of criteria by which a man whose loyalty was unquestioned might still be dismissed as a security risk. It was confidently asserted and certainly hoped that under the new order the public would readily distinguish between the government employee who was fired for disloyalty and the loyal employee who was fired as a security risk. The basic standard in the new order for clearing an employee as a sound security risk is that his *retention* in employment in the federal service is clearly consistent with the interests of national security.

Unhappily the desired differentiation of disloyal employees from innocent security risks very soon dropped out of sight. Perhaps this was to be expected, but the result was certainly made inevitable by the intrusion of politics into the picture. This will be discussed *infra,* p. 198. The net result has been that the same stigma now attaches to the man who is denied security clearance under the new order as formerly attached to the man dismissed for disloyalty. The merging of the two standards in the public mind has been complete, and there have been no effective official efforts to prevent the injustice which has resulted in so many cases.

One point should be made clear. In many areas of government activity where the national security is clearly involved, the right of the government to exercise the widest possible discretion in determining the reliability of those whom it employs cannot be questioned. Precise standards probably cannot be formulated. The man who is denied clearance because he is a security risk for reasons beyond his control is not being "punished" if these "reasons" are made known; but such punishment does result when the dismissal carries, as it now does, the stigma arising from the inferences of disloyalty which seem inevitably to result under the present system. It seems clear that in our program to combat subversion we do, in fact, punish people for misconduct which is so vaguely and loosely defined as to violate in spirit the requirements of certainty demanded by due process of law.

Reference should be made to the use, in one phase of our security program, of standards of loyalty which may be described as "irrelevant," rather than vague. A study by Rowland Watts in 1955 disclosed that the army was dealing with drafted men in the following manner. After a soldier's induction, his entire past life was scrutinized, and if "derogatory" information turned up in his preinduction record, he was given at the end of his term of service an "undesirable discharge" or a "general discharge under honorable conditions" (the Army's way of labeling him "almost subversive"). This was done even if his conduct as a soldier had been immaculate. The injustice of this was so strongly and widely emphasized that the Defense Department has taken some steps toward modifying the policy.

3. Presumptions of Guilt—"Guilt by Association"

The phrase "guilt by association" is in constant use. It is often loosely employed by those who condemn the drawing of any unfavorable inferences from a man's associations with other persons under any circumstances. This of course is nonsense, for there are many instances in which we are bound to consider a man's associations in making various kinds of judgments about him. The whole problem posed by "guilt by association" should be considered against the background of well-established principles in the law which relate to presumptions of guilt. These rules have been developed over the years to protect persons from the injustices resulting from improper presumptions of guilt.

a. *Presumptions of Guilt in Criminal Law*

There are three rules which have emerged here. The first is that guilt is personal. A man cannot be punished for the acts of another person. He may be punished, of course, for conspiracy in planning the acts of other persons, or for inciting another to commit a crime. Second, while a man may be presumed guilty because of inferences drawn from stated facts or conditions, due process of law requires that he be allowed to rebut this presumption of guilt. It might be presumed that a man driving a stolen car had stolen it, but to convict him without allowing him adequate chance to show that he had got it innocently would deny due process. In the third place, in the case of a presumption of guilt there must be a rational connection between a fact and the inference of guilt drawn from it. In 1943 the Supreme Court invalidated a clause of the National Firearms Act which presumed that because a man had in his possession firearms customarily used for crime he must be guilty of the federal offense of transporting them in interstate commerce. The Court found no logical connection here. (*Tot* v. *United States*, 319 U.S. 463.)

In carrying on our program against Communism and subversion, we certainly have frequently violated the last two of the rules relating to presumptions of guilt which the courts have found essential to justice.

b. *Irrebuttable Presumptions of Disloyalty*

In the operation of our program against Communism and subversion there can be no doubt that punishments and disabilities are inflicted upon many persons as the result of presumptions of disloyalty which are in fact irrebuttable. They are irrebuttable for several reasons:

The primary reason is that the procedures of both loyalty and security boards and legislative investigating committees do not provide an assured opportunity to rebut. Security boards are obliged to operate under such rigid security restraints upon disclosing the "confidential" sources and nature of accusations against an employee that in many cases he does not know who is accusing him or the precise charges against him. In many cases the board itself does not know the identity of the accuser.

When legislative committees began investigating subversion their rules of procedure usually afforded no opportunity for a person against whom a presumption of disloyalty had arisen to appear and rebut it. This was intentional, not inadvertent. In 1943 a special committee of the House of Representatives was set up to consider the charges of disloyalty made by Congressman Dies against Messrs. Lovett, Watson, and Dodd (whose dismissal by Congress was later held by the Supreme Court to be a bill of attainder, *supra*, p. 162). This committee refused to hear any witnesses in defense of the three men. Even the agencies which employed the men were not allowed to appear. As one of the committee members remarked, "What could have been accomplished by bringing in every Tom, Dick, and Harry and letting him testify?" This arbitrary attitude no longer prevails, and most committees will try to give a person a chance to rebut accusations or presumptions of disloyalty which have grown out of the committee hearings. But here, as before the security boards, the right to rebut is whittled down by the committee's refusal, in many cases, to disclose the sources of its information or the details of the accusation.

Some investigating committees have indulged in the practice of "citing" long lists of persons as members of suspect or subversive organizations. The Tenney Committee in California did this over a period of years. These persons were not declared to be disloyal; just the fact of membership was noted, and from such "citation" a presumption of disloyalty arose and was intended to arise. What the citation did not note was the time and circumstances of such membership, which, if known, might in many cases have completely rebutted the presumption. There is a clear example of this: The National Council for American-Soviet Friendship was organized early in World War II, to publicize in this country the war effort of our then valued ally, the Soviet Union. It commanded nation-wide support and approval. It held a dinner in New York in 1944 to mark the anniversary of the founding of the Red Army, and Generals Marshall, MacArthur, Pershing, Clark, and Eisenhower all sent messages of congratulation. Later the Attorney General, believing that it had become infiltrated by Communists, listed it as a subversive organization. It is clear that the bald statement by a legislative committee that A was a member or sponsor of the National Council for American-Soviet Friendship creates a presumption of A's disloyalty which he could easily rebut by showing that his membership did not extend beyond the time when all our best generals were praising it. But he gets no opportunity to do this.

Public opinion is heavily responsible for the injustices which arise in cases like this. The public mind has been conditioned to view any accusation of disloyalty as a conclusive finding that a man is disloyal. We are being taught to reason that if a man is accused, he is guilty. His denial will not convince the casual newspaper reader or radio listener that he is free from taint. There must be something wrong with him or no accusation would have arisen. "Cited by the House Committee on Un-American Activities" is a brand he will always carry, whether justly or not.

c. *Illogical Presumptions of Disloyalty*

"Guilt by association" works its gravest injustices when it creates presumptions of disloyalty which have no logical connection with the fact from which the presumption arises. "Guilt by coincidence" is a better term. The prevalence and wide popular acceptance of this type of loose reasoning warrants a close look at it.

(1) *The "fallacy of the undistributed middle."* Anyone familiar with elementary logic is acquainted with the "fallacy of the undistributed middle," and will readily see that the following syllogism is a perfect example of it:

Major premise: Communists condemn Negro discrimination.
Minor premise: Jones condemns Negro discrimination.
Conclusion: Jones is a Communist.

When thus nakedly exposed, the absurdity of this form of reasoning is clear. It has, however, become the stock in trade of many loyalty and security boards, almost all legislative investigating committees, and all private and commercial Communist hunters. The illustrations of its use are countless. One occurred in a national patriotic magazine: "If Communists and left-wingers are against such a bill [the McCarran Immigration and Nationality Bill], then it is safe to say that loyal Americans should be for it." It should be added, however, that too many "coincidences" will properly command attention. They may spell out a pattern of conduct or policy which may validly create presumptions.

This fallacy of "guilt by coincidence" has resulted in putting the brand of disloyalty upon many unquestionably loyal Americans. It has also threatened two of our most cherished American traditions—the right of free public criticism of the officers, policies, and procedures of government and the right of impartial and dispassionate administration of justice. These will now be considered.

(2) *The doctrine of the disloyalty of criticism and dissent.* No one enjoys criticism, and it is a natural human impulse to strike back at one's critics. The doctrine of "guilt by coincidence" seems a ready-made weapon by which those engaged in hunting down and exposing subversives can deal with those who criticize the ruthless and unjust methods sometimes employed. Thus Congressman J. Parnell Thomas, in the early days of the Dies Committee, bluntly stated that anyone who criticized the Committee was "un-American," while the Tenney Committee in California asserted that "the minions of Hitler and Stalin are the ones who want our committee killed."

This is a dangerous threat to one of the basic American traditions of civil liberty—the tradition that the personnel, the policies, and the methods of our government are at all times subject to the full and free criticism of any citizen. To brand as disloyal those who criticize our methods of dealing with the problems of national security, because Communists may also criticize them, is to repudiate the principles of American democracy.

(3) *Threat to the impartial administration of justice.* The fallacious doctrine of "guilt by coincidence" has a frightening impact upon the administration of justice, happily not yet widespread. "Softness" toward communism is an evidence of sympathy for the Communist cause, and it

is but a short step from this to the view that the impartial administration of justice in dealing with Communists adds up to "softness." There has been increasing evidence of the growth of this unhealthy perversion of the principles of justice. When the first trial of Alger Hiss resulted in a hung jury, the trial judge was bitterly attacked on the floor of Congress for judicial conduct stigmatized as "soft" toward Hiss. When Justice Douglas granted a last-minute stay to the Rosenbergs to permit the consideration of a point of law, a member of the House of Representatives introduced a resolution to impeach him. Mention has been made of the judge who imposed unusually heavy penalties upon a Communist for a nonsubversive offense because he was a Communist (*supra,* p. 158). The difficulty in getting non-Communist lawyers to defend persons charged with crimes of subversion reflects in many cases the fear of Communist contagion; there is a growing popular feeling that if as a lawyer you defend a Communist you must share his political views and his disloyalty.

The bar of the country has a clear obligation to combat this threat to the impartial administration of justice.

4. Lack of Procedural Fair Play

Justice Felix Frankfurter has wisely observed, "The history of American freedom is, in no small measure, the history of procedure." Firm insistence upon fair procedure in all governmental operations is the reply of a civilized people to the brutal slogan that "the end justifies the means." The national security will not be jeopardized by according procedural fair play to the most dangerous subversive. Perhaps the most telling criticisms which can validly be brought against our program for combatting communism and subversion are those which are focused on its procedural shortcomings. These procedures are varied, complex, and fluctuating. A detailed analysis of them is beyond the scope of this conspectus, but the following aspects of the problem of procedure deserve inclusion here:

a. *Loyalty and Security Board Procedures*

The procedural safeguards accorded federal employees under the Truman Loyalty Order of 1947, and continued with some modifications under the Eisenhower Security Order of 1953, are more fair and elaborate than those which civil servants have ever enjoyed before. These procedural rights include adequate notice, some indication of charges, the right of counsel, hearing before a presumably impartial loyalty board, the right to introduce evidence and witnesses, and the right to appeal from an adverse decision of the loyalty board. Under the Truman Order this appeal was to the Loyalty Review Board; under the Eisenhower Order it is to the head of the employee's department.

The solid core of the criticism of these procedures is simply stated: the accused or suspected employee has no legal right to a full and accurate statement of all the charges and accusations against him; nor does he have a legal right to know who has accused him, to confront that accuser, and to cross examine him in an effort to establish the truth.

The two rights which are denied here are essential to procedural due process in any criminal prosecution. Hearings before loyalty and security boards are not, however, criminal proceedings regardless of how similar they may seem to the person involved; the denial of these rights, therefore, does not violate the provisions of the Sixth Amendment.

The refusal of the government in loyalty and security hearings to produce its full records, and to bring in its informers and witnesses, is not to be attributed to a wanton and malicious desire to treat these federal employees unjustly. It stems rather from the conviction of responsible officials that the national security does not permit either the production of complete FBI files relating to accused employees or the disclosure of the identity of those who have given information to the government, let alone their cross examination.

In this dilemma between security and procedural justice, the position of the government should be understood. The FBI, and other investigating agencies, get much of their information about loyalty and security suspects from confidential sources. These may be secret informers or undercover agents. In either case their usefulness in securing information would cease if their identities were disclosed, and the production of the full texts of FBI reports would usually reveal who had provided the information contained.

Against these considerations of security may be placed the belief, strongly held by many, that the government does not do what it reasonably could in producing specific accusations and witnesses. It hides, rather, behind a plea of security which in very many instances is not well grounded. Many find it hard to believe that the national security requires the government *never* to reveal the identity of *any* accuser.

From these same considerations of national security stems the policy followed by some security boards of refusing to state the grounds upon which an employee is dismissed as a security risk. The hardship and injustice resulting from this can be very serious.

In October, 1955, the United States Court of Appeals in California held that a seaman was denied due process of law when he was barred on security grounds by the United States Coast Guard from employment on a merchant vessel without notice and a hearing at which he could confront adverse witnesses. *(Parker* v. *Lester,* 227 Fed. 2d 708.) The Coast Guard was enforcing the security provisions of the Magnuson Act of 1950. The government announced it would not appeal the case.

b. *Procedures of Legislative Investigating Committees*

Only the more important aspects of the committee procedure problem can be discussed.

While Congress has full authority over the procedures of its committees, until very recently the committees were left to their own judgment in this important matter. Mr. J. Parnell Thomas, while chairman of the House Committee on Un-American Activities, told an obstreperous lawyer who was serving a witness before the Committee, "The rights you have are the rights given you by this committee. We will determine what rights you have and what rights you have not got before the committee." This may have been indiscreet, but it was frank realism, and until fairly recently it accurately stated the facts. For unless Congress does something about it, an investigating committee is a law unto itself, and unless the committee does something about it, the chairman is pretty much a law unto himself.

It was in the context of this complete freedom from restraints upon their behavior that federal and state committees investigating subversion began their work. The degree of procedural abuses evident in committee hearings varied with the problems being investigated, the behavior of the witnesses, and the personality of committee chairman. It may be noted that if the committees were sometimes brutal and arbitrary in their treatment of witnesses, there were plenty of witnesses who tried to browbeat and obstruct the committee.

(1) *Abuses in legislative committee procedures.* While the list is not exhaustive, the following are the more important abuses which became embedded in the procedures of these committees. They have not occurred all the time, nor have they all been present at once in any legislative investigation.

(a) *Denial of the traditional rights of witnesses.* Committees are free to follow their own whims in dealing with witnesses, and since these inquiries into subversion are often in reality "legislative trials," denial of the rights traditionally guaranteed to witnesses, not to mention defendants, works serious injustice. Among these rights may be listed the right to adequate notice of the hearing, with some indication of its purpose; sufficient time to secure counsel and the right to the advice of counsel at the hearing; the right to make a statement which shall become part of the record; the right to testify freely and to explain his answers to questions asked of him; the right to reply fully to charges or accusations made against him; the right to a transcript at reasonable expense of his own testimony. Investigating committees, like loyalty and security boards, have refused to disclose the full text of accusations made by confidential informers and to produce these anonymous accusers in open hearing. The injustice and hardship resulting from this refusal may be extremely serious.

(b) *Abuses of publicity.* Committees investigating subversion have usually conducted their open hearings in a blaze of publicity. This publicity has often been nation-wide through newspaper reports, radio, and even television. It is a disputed point whether this goldfish-bowl publicity can be regarded as an invasion of the rights of a witness who shrinks from it. It is a serious injustice, however, for a committee to give this nation-wide publicity in advance to accusations, insinuations, or suspicions directed against a person who frequently is not accorded a fair opportunity to answer back and whose defense, if he has one, will never catch up with the original headlines accusing him. Committees have sometimes misused publicity in another way. After a witness has testified in a secret session of the committee, the chairman, or other member, has released to the press selected parts of this secret testimony. The witness is sometimes unfairly or inadequately presented to the public in this way and the resulting injustice may be very great.

(c) *"Name-dropping" by "friendly witnesses."* Investigating committees frequently seek the aid of professional informers, usually ex-Communists, from whom much valuable information about the Communist movement has been secured. The propriety of taking advantage of this information seems clear. The committees, however, sometimes use these informers in ways which cannot be so easily defended. They appear as "friendly" witnesses, testify publicly, and often without interruption or cross examination, sprinkling the record with the names of persons whom they accuse as, or whom they suspect of being, Communists or subversives. Persons who are the victims of this irresponsible "name-dropping" may be entirely innocent. The committee may or may not allow them to appear to refute the charges against their loyalty; but even if it does, the damage is often irremediable.

(d) *One-man committee hearings.* Committee hearings conducted by the chairman alone, or by any single member, date back to the days of the Dies Committee. Some of the most flagrant invasions of the witnesses' right to essential fair play have occurred in these one-man hearings. Uninhibited by any restraining influence exerted by the presence of his colleagues, this one man, who for the time being *is* the committee, may indulge in tactics which would not be tolerated by the full committee.

(e) *Allowing improper use of committee files.* The files assembled by legislative investigating committees are official government records. They are the property of the government, to be used in the official work of the committee or other agencies of the government. These files contain information about thousands of individuals, some of it reliable, some of it admittedly unsifted and therefore unreliable. The House Committee on Un-American Activities from time to time allowed access to its files, or released information from its files, to persons not connected with the government. Some of these persons were private or commercial Communist-hunters, newspapermen, or radio broadcasters. Such bootlegging of the contents of official, confidential documents inflicts a serious injustice upon those whose names are thus improperly released to outsiders. In the light of this evidence of committee irresponsibility one can understand the adamant opposition of the President, the Attorney General, and Mr. J. Edgar Hoover to demands that FBI records be turned over to congressional committees.

(2) *The problem of improving committee procedures.* The proposals for improving the procedures of legislative committees investigating subversion have been too numer-

ous and too varied to be analyzed here. The following points may be made, however, regarding this diversified program for reform:

First, the reform will not be imposed upon the committees by the courts. These hearings are not judicial or even quasi-judicial proceedings. They are, supposedly, legislative efforts to get information. The courts have thus far shown little disposition to tell Congress how the hearings should be run or to suggest that committee procedures must meet some test of fairness required by the due process clause of the Fifth Amendment.

Second, Congress has full authority to establish proper rules of procedure for its committees and to enforce compliance with such rules. Congress is a political body, and therefore sensitive to changes in public opinion. In 1954 the American Bar Association by a heavy vote proposed important changes in congressional investigative procedure, designed to correct most of the abuses just discussed. Such action can hardly fail to have influence. There are substantial improvements in the present conduct of congressional investigating committees, and there is a growing probability that Congress itself may take effective action.

In short, the solution of this problem will be found, if at all, in the establishment not of judicially enforceable rules but of sound mores supported by a public opinion which demands fair play.

5. "Justice by Politicians" in Our Program against Subversion

A basic principle of law and justice demands that a man be tried for crime before an impartial judge. The law does not regard a judge as impartial if he stands to profit from the conviction of those tried in his court. In the Tumey case, in 1927 (*Tumey* v. *Ohio*, 273 U.S. 510), the Supreme Court held that due process of law was denied to persons tried for crime before a judge whose compensation was increased (by the amount of the court costs) if they were convicted rather than acquitted. It would be equally a denial of justice if the judge gained politically, rather than financially, by convicting as many people as possible.

It was probably inescapable that our program for combatting communism and subversion should have fallen into the hands of politicians, or into the hands of men who must work under the domination of politicians. Basic policies affecting the national security must naturally be established by Congress. But the task of "punitive exposure" of subversives assumed by our congressional investigating committees is a very different matter. To place the reputations and livelihood of persons accused or suspected of disloyalty in the hands of men whose political fortunes are directly enhanced by the number of persons thus "exposed" as disloyal is to violate basic principles of fair play.

That political ambitions have heavily influenced important phases of our campaign to protect our national security is not open to question. For some years the hunting down and exposing of Communists and subversives has been the most profitable activity, politically, in which a congressman can engage. It is reported that when, in 1953, the Eighty-Third Congress was organized, 185 of 221 Republican members of the House of Representatives applied for membership on the House Committee on Un-American Activities. Such membership offered the best chance of getting into the political limelight and staying there.

The intrusion of politics into our program to combat subversion has intensified, if it did not generate, some of the abuses and injustices which have marred that program. The political value of publicity does not need to be argued, and therefore congressional committees investigating disloyalty have operated whenever possible in a blaze of publicity—publicity so helpful to the political fortunes of the committee members, so damaging in many cases to the rights of those investigated. It is also clear that if political fortunes are to be made by "exposing" Communists and subversives, it would be unfortunate to have the supply run out. And this may well have an effect upon the standards by which an investigating committee judges the loyalty of a man. Perhaps this explains why the House Committee on Un-American Activities could list 624 subversive organizations in 1951, when the Attorney General, implementing the Loyalty Order, could find only about 200.

The political dividends paid to a great many people by the operation of our program against communism has created an atmosphere of great ruthlessness toward anything remotely suggesting disloyalty. No public official can afford to risk being branded as "soft" toward communism. It is not, however, being "soft" toward communism to point out that this atmosphere is a very unhealthy one in which to carry on what ought to be the judicial, or quasi-judicial, job of determining the loyalty or disloyalty of individual human beings. It would be strange indeed if the members of our many security boards in federal civil service and in the armed forces were not acutely conscious of this atmosphere, and even stranger if they were not somewhat affected by it.

These political motives operate with great vigor on the state and local level. We have an impressive arsenal of state legislation directed against communism, subversion, and sedition. It is very doubtful whether the national security really demands all this, although prudent and efficient aid from the states is desirable. What appears to be going on, however, is a sort of competition amongst many of the states to see which can pass the toughest legislation against communism. It is equally clear that the authors of these harsh laws earn political prestige in their own states and sometimes in the nation. And to become the chairman of an important state legislative committee on un-American activities is to become a national figure.

What has been said here is not an attack on politicians, or on politics. Robert A. Lovett aptly observed that the word "politician is a job description, not an epithet," and we could not do without politicians. But serious injustices will result when politicians are put at the task of punishing people they decide are disloyal, even if the punishment is euphemistically called "exposure."

6. Private Efforts to Combat Communism and Subversion—"Vigilantism"

The zeal of some citizens in any community to concern themselves with the patriotism and loyalty of their neighbors is a very old and very human impulse. In addition, it is the clear duty of a citizen to aid in the enforcement of law by reporting any evidence of crime which comes to his attention. For these and perhaps other reasons, there has been a mushroom growth during the period of the cold war of groups and organizations which have claimed a share in the nation's drive against communism and subversion. Neither the groups nor their activities can be analyzed in detail, but the results of their efforts may be classified roughly as follows:

a. *Private Loyalty Oaths*

One of the strange phenomena of recent years is the spread, like a contagion, of loyalty oath requirements in private organizations. A tabulation of them would run into the hundreds. Even the Gold Star Mothers now require a loyalty oath of their members.

In membership organizations, social, religious, civic, or otherwise, it is difficult to see what these oaths accomplish beyond the ostracism of some stubborn person who refuses to take the oath and is thereupon rejected or ejected. To this should probably be added the emotional stimulation of those in the organization who evidenced their patriotism by requiring the oath.

Where employment or other economic rights or advantages are involved the oath requirement may have the same consequences as the oaths required by state or local governments. (*Supra,* p. 174.)

No case is yet on record of an avowed Communist who was identified by his refusal to take a loyalty oath. Nor is there knowledge of an attempt to punish in any way anyone who has falsely taken a loyalty oath required by a private organization.

b. *Civic and Patriotic Groups Which Combat Communism and Disloyalty*

There are many organizations, some with very large memberships, which devote time, money, and effort to patriotic endeavors, among which anti-Communist activity is high on the list. Here may be mentioned the American Legion and the DAR. Some groups do nothing but engage in efforts directed against subversive or "leftist" influences.

These are pressure groups, and their influence is in proportion to their size. The American Legion can make its influence felt in the corridors of many a state capitol, and its influence is not negligible in Washington. Pressure is brought by these organizations upon state legislatures to enact tough anti-Communist legislation. It is brought upon schools and colleges to dismiss teachers whose loyalty has been challenged, and upon school boards to bar the use in the schools of textbooks of which the organization does not approve. Much of this activity may threaten First Amendment rights of free thought and expression. It is, however, the kind of activity that any group of citizens who has energy enough may engage in, and it is an activity which is open and aboveboard. Public opinion is always free to combat public opinion.

c. *Commercial Communist-Hunters—Blacklisting*

A number of organizations now exist which engage on a strictly business basis in searching the loyalty of individuals and selling their findings to any interested buyer. If a business house wishes to be assured that its employees are immaculate in the matter of loyalty, there are a number of organizations which will do a sort of "Dun and Bradstreet" loyalty check for an appropriate fee. One organization in New York claims to have in its files the names of nearly a million and a half persons against whom there exists some "derogatory information." The identity of any of these can be purchased.

The anti-Communist newsletters, such as *Counterattack,* assemble and sell to subscribers information relating to the loyalty of persons and organizations. This is a service regarded as very valuable by many businessmen anxious to avoid any possible "leftist" or "pink" contamination.

Out of these commercialized loyalty screenings the "blacklist" has emerged. The names of persons found by these commercial Communist-hunters to be disloyal or in any way suspect are compiled, and such lists may be purchased by employers or others wishing to have them. Of course, those who compile such a list have no power to hire or fire the persons on it. But business concerns have shown themselves very sensitive to the implied suggestion that it would be better from a "public relations" standpoint not to employ these "disloyal," "suspect," or "controversial" persons on the list. It is so simple to avoid trouble or criticism in this way. The best-known list of this sort was the booklet *Red Channels,* issued by the publishers of *Counterattack* in 1950. *Red Channels* is simply a list of some 150 people in the entertainment industry, and after each name appears a list of all the organizations and associations of a suspect nature to which the person belonged, compiled from the Attorney General's list and the reports of various legislative investigating committees. It contained no accusations, merely "citations" drawn from official sources. It did not itself "blacklist" anyone, but it could be used, and was, by some advertisers and sponsors as a blacklist. An actor or radio artist listed in *Red Channels* became a "controversial" figure in the eyes of many possible sponsors too busy to worry about whether the listed person was in reality disloyal. The whole problem of "blacklisting" is complex and merits careful study.

These private efforts to combat communism and subversion, unless carried on with prudence and tolerance, are a deviation from our traditional principles of justice and fair play. They very easily degenerate into vigilante activity, which cannot be defended in a community based upon law and order. Private justice is irresponsible justice, which, in essence, is injustice.

SELECTED READINGS

Two important collections of source materials on the subject of this section are: *Internal Security Manual* (Senate Document No. 40, 84th Cong., 1st Sess., 1955), which contains statutes, executive orders, and congressional resolutions relating to internal security; and *Digest of the Public Record of Communism in the United States* (New York: Fund for the Republic, 1955), which contains "digests or extracts of public records of the most significant executive action, legislation, and legislative committee proceedings, and court proceedings" relevant to the Communist problem in the United States.

There are many books and documents which set out and analyze the Communist threat to our internal security. Among these are: Nathaniel Weyl, *The Battle against Disloyalty* (New York: Crowell, 1953); Edward E. Palmer (editor), *The Communist Problem in America: A Book of Readings* (New York: Crowell, 1951); James Burnham, *The Web of Subversion: Underground Networks in the United States Government* (New York: John Day, 1954); *The Red Exposure: A Study of Subversive Influences* (Indianapolis: American Legion, 1948); William H. Chamberlin, *America's Second Crusade* (Chicago: Henry Regnery, 1950); James Rorty and Moshe Decter, *McCarthy and the Communists* (Boston: Beacon Press, 1954); Herbert A. Philbrick, *I Led Three Lives: Citizen, "Communist," Counter-Spy* (New York: McGraw-Hill, 1952); Whitaker Chambers, *Witness* (New York: Random House, 1952). There are numerous government publications, such as *The Communist Party of the United States of America: Handbook for Americans* (Subcommittee on Internal Security of Senate Committee on the Judiciary, 84th Cong., 1st Sess., 1955), as well as hearings and reports by this committee and others. There have been numerous reports by the House Committee on Un-American Activities. The Government Printing Office will mail upon request a price list of all government publications relating to Communism and subversion available for sale at that office.

Books dealing in a general way with the impact on civil liberties of the government's measures for the protection of internal security include: Francis Biddle, *The Fear of Freedom* (New York: Doubleday, 1951); Alan Barth, *The Loyalty of Free Men* (New York: Viking Press, 1951); Harold D. Lasswell, *National Security and Individual Freedom* (New York: McGraw-Hill, 1950); Henry S. Commager, *Freedom, Loyalty, Dissent* (New York: Oxford University Press, 1954); John Lord O'Brian, *National Security and Individual Freedom* (Cambridge: Harvard University Press, 1955).

Samuel A. Stouffer, *Communism, Conformity and Civil Liberties—A Cross-Section of the Nation Speaks Its Mind* (New York: Doubleday, 1955), presents conclusions, based on careful and extensive polls, on the attitude of public opinion toward the Communist threat and allied topics.

The following books deal with the loyalty and security programs: Eleanor Bontecou, *The Federal Loyalty-Security Program* (Ithaca: Cornell University Press, 1952); Walter Gellhorn, *Security, Loyalty and Science* (Ithaca: Cornell University Press, 1950); Walter Gellhorn (editor), *The States and Subversion* (Ithaca: Cornell University Press, 1952); Alan Westin, *The Constitution and Loyalty Programs* (New York: Carrie Chapman Catt Memorial Fund, Inc., 1954). Adam Yarmolinsky, *Case Studies in Personal Security* (Washington: Bureau of National Affairs, 1955), presents reports on fifty security cases based on the files of the attorneys who acted for the employees involved. Rowland Watts, *The Draftee and Internal Security: A Study of the Army Military Personnel Program* and *Appendix* (New York: Workers Defense League, 1955), analyzes the security procedures used by the Army in dealing with drafted men. All these books are in varying degrees critical of the loyalty and security programs. There are as yet no comparable studies defending the programs.

There are useful books dealing with the legislative committees that investigate communism and subversion. Among them are: August R. Ogden, *The Dies Committee: A Study of the Special House Committee for the Investigation of Un-American Activities, 1938-1944* (Washington: Catholic University of America Press, 2d ed., 1945); Robert K. Carr, *The House Committee on Un-American Activities, 1945-1950* (Ithaca: Cornell University Press, 1952); Edward L. Barrett, *The Tenney Committee: Legislative Investigation of Subversive Activities in California* (Ithaca: Cornell University Press, 1951); Lawrence H. Chamberlain, *Loyalty and Legislative Action: A Survey of Activity by the New York State Legislature, 1919-1949* (Ithaca: Cornell University Press, 1951).

More recent and more general are Alan Barth, *Government by Investigation* (New York: Viking Press, 1955); Telford Taylor, *The Grand Inquest: The Story of Congressional Investigations* (New York: Simon and Schuster, 1955).

William F. Buckley, Jr., and L. Brent Bozell, *McCarthy and His Enemies: The Record and Its Meaning* (Chicago: Henry Regnery, 1954), is an able defense of a controversial investigating committee chairman. See also James Rorty and Moshe Decter, *McCarthy and the Communists* (Boston: Beacon Press, 1954).

The House Committee on Un-American Activities has issued annual reports and many special reports in which the purposes and achievements of the Committee are presented. In some of these reports criticisms directed against the Committee are answered. There are similar reports of the Senate Subcommittee on Internal Security. Many of these documents are available either from the committees or from the Government Printing Office.

·VIII·

Civil Liberties of Aliens

THE civil liberties of aliens have to be viewed in the light of the fact that there is no constitutional provision or any rule of international law which requires us to admit any alien, and we can go very far in dictating the terms upon which we allow him to remain here. A good many aspects of our immigration and deportation policies reflect this consciousness of a discretionary power to deal with aliens as we please. Obviously the rights of aliens in this country are protected by a large number of treaties we have with other countries; but not all aliens are so protected, and those who are not are subject to many restrictions and disabilities not visited upon citizens.

Aliens are ineligible to take a federal civil service examination, and the statutes of the states are full of provisions which bar noncitizens from a long list of licensed occupations and professions. The Supreme Court held many years ago, in *Truax* v. *Raich* (239 U.S. 33, 1915), that a state might not, however, set up such restrictions as would bar aliens from the chance to earn a livelihood.

In 1920 California forbade the ownership of land by aliens ineligible to citizenship (most of whom were Chinese or Japanese), and in 1921 Washington barred from land ownership aliens who had not declared intention to become citizens, a group which would include "ineligible" aliens. These laws were upheld by the Supreme Court against the charge of denial of equal protection of the laws. *(Porterfield v. Webb,* 263 U.S. 225, 1923; *Terrace v. Thompson,* 263 U.S. 197, 1923.)More recently doubt has been cast upon the validity of these alien land laws by the Supreme Court's decision in 1948 *(Takahashi v. Fish and Game Commission,* 334 U.S. 410) that the equal protection clause was violated by a California statute denying commercial fishing licenses to ineligible aliens. Since the 1948 decision state supreme courts in Oregon and California have held that state alien land laws deny equal protection. *(Namba et al. v. McCourt,* 185 Ore. 579, 1949; *Sei Fujii v. State,* 242 Pac. 2d 617, 1952.)

The Immigration and Nationality Act of 1952 was sharply attacked for its discrimination against South-European and Asian peoples through its continuance of the so-called quota system. President Truman vetoed the bill on this ground among others, but it was passed over his veto. He declared that immigration from these areas of the world would be "reduced to a trickle." There have been persistent efforts in Congress and out to bring about such an amendment to the Act as would correct the provisions believed to be unjust and discriminatory. These efforts have not so far met with any success.

The Act of 1952 stiffened harshly the conditions under which an alien might secure a visa, not to enter this country for permanent residence, but merely for a temporary visit. Many of these conditions relate to the applicant's political views and the possibility that he might while in the United States be in any sense a threat to our national security. These provisions have become controversial, not because there is any desire to have dangerous aliens admitted but because of the rather arbitrary administration of the rules by American officials abroad and here at home who perhaps were fearful of being thought "soft" toward communism and subversion. The problem has been highlighted by the numerous refusals of the State Department to admit to this country as temporary visitors some of the most distinguished scientists, artists, and men of letters in the world. Several scientific congresses scheduled to be held in this country were canceled because of the inability of guest scientists to secure visas allowing them to come.

The provisions of the Internal Security Act of 1950 and of the Immigration and Nationality Act of 1952 directed against alien subversion have been mentioned *supra,* p. 168.

SELECTED READINGS

A useful background for the study of current problems affecting the alien is found in William S. Bernard (editor), *American Immigration Policy—A Reappraisal* (New York: Harper, 1950), published under the sponsorship of the National Committee on Immigration Policy.

The civil liberties of aliens are presently governed by the McCarran-Walter Act of 1952, about which much controversy still rages. The considerations which led to the passage of the Act are set out in *The Immigration and Naturalization Systems of the United States,* Report of the Senate Committee on the Judiciary, pursuant to S. 137, 80th Cong., 1st Sess., 1950. This committee has held hearings and published reports on other, narrower phases of the problem.

Critical of the McCarran-Walter Act are the following: *Whom Shall We Welcome?* (Commission on Immigration and Naturalization: Government Printing Office, 1953); Milton R. Konvitz, *Civil Rights on Immigration* (Ithaca: Cornell University Press, 1953).

· IX ·

Racial Discrimination

A. DISCRIMINATION AGAINST NEGROES

1. Status at the End of World War II

A SURVEY of the status of the civil liberties and rights of the American Negro at the close of World War II brings to light the following facts:

(a) There were no striking changes in the patterns of Negro segregation in the South, although in some communities Negroes were admitted to some jobs previously closed to them, and interracial relations were increasingly friendly.

(b) Segregation was still maintained in the armed forces of the United States, although encouraging progress had been made in the Navy. Some efforts had been made during the war to deal with this problem and to improve the position of the Negro, and although one or two experiments in integration of Negro and white troops had given reassuring results, nothing substantial was accomplished on a permanent basis.

(c) The early cases which had upheld the validity of

racial discrimination in the form of restrictive convenants in private housing were undisturbed.

(d) Washington, D.C., the capital of the greatest democratic nation in the world, was still a Jim Crow city in spite of the complete authority of Congress to eliminate racial segregation there.

(e) The wartime Fair Employment Practices Committee had proved a very valuable and healthy experiment. The belief that a nation at war could not defend failure to use available manpower because it was colored had led to the establishment of a program under which many business concerns producing war materials were persuaded to abandon previous policies of racial discrimination. Compliance here was not one hundred per cent, but it was very impressive, and perhaps the most important consequence of the experiment was the striking evidence which it produced that racial conflict and violence did not result from putting Negroes and whites at work in the same factories. The railroad industry, however, stubbornly resisted the employment of Negroes as conductors, engineers, and so forth.

(f) In 1944 came the important Supreme Court decision, *Smith* v. *Allwright*. (321 U.S. 649.) This outlawed the so-called "white primary" in the South, which was the last effective legal device by which southern states could continue any open and aboveboard program of Negro disfranchisement.

(g) A good many northern communities came to grips for the first time with race tensions on a sizable scale. Negro laborers had been brought north to work in war plants, and communities of the North became more race conscious than they had been before.

2. Developments since 1945

a. *Civil Rights Program of 1946*

In December, 1946, President Truman created the President's Committee on Civil Rights, composed of a group of distinguished citizens under the chairmanship of Mr. Charles E. Wilson of General Electric. The staff work was under the direction of Professor Robert K. Carr of Dartmouth College. While the committee dealt broadly with problems of civil rights, one of its chief concerns was with the problems relating to Negro discrimination and segregation, and some of its main proposals were directed toward the possible solution of these problems and more adequate education of public opinion with respect to them.

One of the Committee's most controversial proposals was for a peacetime Fair Employment Practices program. President Truman supported the conclusions and recommendations of the Committee in a legislative program submitted to Congress which became dubbed the "President's Civil Rights Program." It aroused wide and bitter debate. It was defeated largely by the solid opposition of the southern Senators, and the President's endorsement of it led to a serious split in the Democratic Party. Nevertheless, while the program produced no concrete results, it did contribute to public education with respect to civil rights problems, and the report of the President's Committee placed before the country a memorable statement of ideals.

President Truman sought to keep alive after the close of the war this policy of antidiscrimination in government contracts through the agency of the President's Committee on Government Contract Compliance. The net accomplishments, save for some research, were pretty meager. President Eisenhower has continued and strengthened the Committee under the chairmanship of the Vice President. It has a larger staff and is carrying on a fairly dynamic program of education and conciliation.

b. *Racially Restrictive Covenants*

There is no provision of the federal Constitution which forbids the practice of racial discrimination by private individuals. In the area of housing or the establishment of residential areas, the practice had grown up and had been held valid of excluding members of the Negro race or other races from privately controlled developments through the device of restrictive covenants written into leases and deeds of sale. *(Corrigan* v. *Buckley,* 271 U.S. 323, 1926.) This practice had been believed to be beyond the reach of any law. In 1948, however, came the Supreme Court decisions in *Shelley* v. *Kraemer* (334 U.S. 1) and *Hurd* v. *Hodge* (334 U.S. 24) holding that while racially restrictive covenants were not in themselves unlawful, they were unenforceable in any court of law, federal or state. To permit a state court to enforce one of the restrictive agreements made the state a party to the discrimination involved and brought it therefore under the prohibitions of the Fourteenth Amendment. In 1953 the Supreme Court bolstered this important rule by holding that a restrictive covenant may not be enforced by a suit for damages against the white co-covenanter who broke the covenant. *(Barrows* v. *Jackson,* 346 U.S. 249.) In short, restrictive covenants became merely gentlemen's agreements which could persist only as long as the parties to them felt bound to observe them.

The practical importance of these decisions can be exaggerated, for in most areas from which Negroes are now barred as the results of these gentlemen's agreements they will probably continue to be barred, at least for some time to come. The cases created for the Negro no positive rights; they merely deprived those who discriminate against him of the use of state or federal courts in doing so.

c. *State Antidiscrimination Laws*

A number of northern states have long had laws on their statute books forbidding racial discrimination in the enjoyment of public and semipublic facilities, whereas the laws in the southern states have made such segregation mandatory. These northern statutes apply mainly to transportation facilities, hotels, restaurants, places of amusement, and the like. They are usually enforceable by means of suits for damages which can be brought by Negroes against those who practice the discrimination.

In the forefront of this legislation the state of New York in the Ives-Quinn Act of 1945 forbade discrimination based upon race, color, or religion in employment throughout the state, and it created an antidiscrimination commission to enforce the law by the issuance of cease and desist orders with ultimate court review. Later the New York legislature forbade racial and religious discrimination in tax-supported schools and universities or in any institutions under the control of the Regents. Misgivings that this legislation moved too far in advance of public opinion were needless. Compliance with the laws, as in the case of FEPC during the war, has come about very substantially through negotiation and voluntary compliance, with resort to court action almost nonexistent.

Fifteen states have enacted legislation in this area. The provisions vary from state to state, but in only three of the fifteen states are the antidiscrimination laws voluntary in nature. In twelve states governmental machinery exists for bringing about compliance. The operation of these statutes has on the whole been reassuring; many of these communities have adjusted themselves to the employment of Negroes in work from which they had previously been barred.

An increasing number of cities, including Philadelphia, Pittsburgh, and Chicago, have ordinances forbidding racial job discrimination.

d. *Segregation in the District of Columbia*

Segregation persisted in the District of Columbia, owing to the fact that the District was carved out of the southern states of Virginia and Maryland, and the native population of the District inherited the traditions of southern communities on this problem. Congress itself has taken no legislative action with respect to segregation in the District. In 1953, however, the Supreme Court unanimously held valid and in full force an act passed in 1873 by the Legislative Assembly of the District which made it a crime to discriminate against a person on grounds of race or color in any restaurant or other eating place. *(District of Columbia v. Thompson Co.,* 346 U.S. 100.) The District enjoyed a measure of self-government at that time. The Court held the Act could not be deemed abandoned or replaced as a result of nonuse. Since this decision, and since the Court's school segregation decision *(Bolling v. Sharpe,* 347 U.S. 497, 1954), the end of segregation in the District seems clearly in sight.

e. *Segregation in Interstate Transportation*

Congress has been equally reluctant to act in the field of interstate transportation. Under the delegated power to regulate interstate commerce Congress could abolish by law all forms of segregation on interstate trains or other modes of interstate transportation. Furthermore, the Supreme Court of the United States has held that Congress is the only authority which can do this. Shortly after the Civil War it held invalid a state statute which forbade Negro segregation on steamboats moving up and down the Mississippi River *(Hall* v. *DeCuir,* 95 U.S. 485, 1878), and in 1946 it held invalid a Virginia statute requiring Negro segregation on interstate buses passing through the state *(Morgan* v. *Commonwealth of Virginia,* 328 U.S. 373, 1946). In both cases the Court held that the problem of segregation or nonsegregation on interstate carriers was a federal problem and that attempts by individual states to deal with it were invalid obstructions of interstate commerce.

Federal policy with respect to segregation on interstate carriers is grounded on a section of the Interstate Commerce Act of 1887, as amended in 1940, which forbids railroads in interstate commerce "to subject any particular person... to any undue or unreasonable prejudice or disadvantage in any respect whatsoever...." The Interstate Commerce Commission had taken the attitude—under pressure, it must be said, from the courts—that racial discrimination in interstate commerce violates the statute. Discrimination in this context, however, had been defined in terms of the doctrine of *Plessy* v. *Ferguson* (163 U.S. 537), in 1896, that a railroad which provides "separate but equal" accommodations to passengers was held not to be violating the Act.

In 1950 the Supreme Court in the Henderson case held that the long-established practice of the Pullman Company of setting aside and curtaining off three or four seats in a dining car for the exclusive use of Negroes did in fact amount to discrimination. *(Henderson v. United States,* 339 U.S. 816.)

In November, 1955, the Interstate Commerce Commission issued a sweeping order banning segregation on interstate trains and buses and in public waiting rooms serving interstate travelers. The Commission cited the Supreme Court's 1954 decision in the school segregation cases *(infra,* p. 221) in support of its order.

f. *The "Separate but Equal" rule of* Plessy v. Ferguson

Between 1945 and the 1954 Supreme Court decision in the school segregation cases, judicial rulings on the problems of Negro segregation were mainly a continuance and tightening of the judicial standards of equality under segregation. The old 1896 rule of *Plessy* v. *Ferguson* that equal but separate accommodations did not deny equal protection of the law still prevailed.

The problem came up mainly in the cases in the field of higher education.

(1) *The Gaines case.* In 1938 *(Missouri* ex rel. *Gaines* v. *Canada,* 305 U.S. 337) the Court held that a Negro who wished to study law in a state which had a state-supported law school for white students was entitled to admission either to that school or to an equally adequate state-supported Negro law school.

(2) *The Sipuel case.* In 1948 *(Sipuel* v. *University of Oklahoma,* 332 U.S. 631), however, the Court bore down more sharply on the southern states. It held that a prospective Negro law student not only was entitled to be admitted to a Negro law school equal in quality to the state's white law school, but was also entitled to have his appli-

cation for admission acted upon as promptly as that of any white student. He could not, in other words, be asked to wait while the state built the law school.

(3) *The Sweatt case.* In 1950 *(Sweatt* v. *Painter,* 339 U.S. 629) the Court came very close to reversing the doctrine of *Plessy* v. *Ferguson.* It held that a separate Negro law school set up in Texas under much more favorable circumstances than had prevailed in any other southern state did not meet the test of equality required by the Fourteenth Amendment and that this failure was in the main the result of the very fact of segregation. In other words, law students isolated from other law students could not for that very reason receive as good a legal education as would be possible if they were all in the same school.

Virtually all of the segregation cases during this period dealt with education in the colleges and universities, especially the professional and graduate schools. Many of the southern states recognized the impossibility of providing duplicate professional and educational facilities for Negro and white students and met the impact of these decisions by abandoning Negro segregation in graduate schools. This could be done without serious social upheaval, because of the limited number of Negro students who would at any one time have to be assimilated into southern colleges and universities; but this was, as time has shown, no index of the willingness of a southern state to make this concession in its elementary schools, where in many instances the number of Negro children was far greater than that of the whites.

g. *Discrimination in Public and Tax-exempt Housing*

The development during and after the war of large-scale housing projects, financed in some cases directly by the government and in some cases by private capital on a tax-exempt basis, was bound to bring to the surface acute problems of racial discrimination. If the taxpayers' money is being spent through loans, direct subsidies, or tax exemptions for housing projects, it is hard to see how the exclusion from these housing projects of people on purely racial grounds can be defended.

A close case was that of *Dorsey* v. *Stuyvesant Town Corp.* (299 N.Y. 512, 1949). Here the Stuyvesant Town development in New York City, financed by the Metropolitan Life Insurance Company, received partial tax exemption from the city, although it was known that Negroes would be excluded from the housing project. The entire cost of acquisition and construction was met by the corporation. Negroes were excluded, and the New York Court of Appeals held that the discrimination was not the act of the state but of the company and did not, therefore, violate the equal protection clause. The tax exemption seemed unimportant to the court. The Supreme Court denied certiorari, Justices Black and Douglas dissenting. (339 U.S. 981, 1950.)

h. *Discrimination in the Armed Forces*

Both Presidents Truman and Eisenhower, as well as the Department of Defense, were determined, after the war, to eliminate the color line in the armed services as promptly as possible. This policy was pushed forward until segregation as a deliberate policy has virtually disappeared. There has been integration of white and colored men serving in the armed services, elimination of segregation from the schools on army posts and similar establishments, and the breaking down of barriers, both formal and informal, which had previously made it almost impossible for Negroes to secure promotions as easily as white officers. Naturally, in an organization as enormous as our defense establishment there will always remain the opportunity for individual officers to drag their feet in complying with the principle that Negroes are to receive the same treatment as whites.

i. *General Improvement of Race Relations*

The period after World War II was one of quiet and widespread gains in the field of better race relations. Charles Johnson's book *Into the Main Stream* undertakes to point up the various ways in which these gains were brought about and the promises which they hold. The importance of this is very considerable. A lynching, a race riot such as occurred in Cicero, Illinois, or some other ugly demonstration of racial antagonism is sure to be played up by the press and obscure the extent to which in many communities all over the country, north and south, Negroes and whites are associating together on terms of equality and mutual respect without any friction of any sort.

3. THE SCHOOL SEGREGATION CASES OF 1954

In the cases brought before the Supreme Court prior to 1952 the Court was able to avoid facing the issue of the constitutionality of segregation, *per se,* and was still able to assume without needing to reaffirm the "separate but equal" doctrine laid down in *Plessy* v. *Ferguson,* discussed on page 218 above. But in the five school segregation cases brought to the Court in 1952 there was no opportunity to evade longer the constitutional issue of segregation *per se.* The Court accepted as the basis for decision that the school facilities extended to Negro and white children under segregation in these cases were equal or were being equalized in quality and character, and the only point raised was whether segregation in and of itself violated the equal protection clause.

The Court heard argument on this important issue in the fall of 1952. At the very end of the term the Court restored the case for reargument at the following term, and asked counsel (who included the Department of Justice) to present briefs and arguments on several specific questions. One was the question whether there was historical evidence which would throw light upon the intentions of the framers of the Fourteenth Amendment, or of the state legislatures which ratified it, with respect to its possible application to segregation in the public schools. Argument was also asked upon the kind of decree which the Court might hand down, assuming that it should hold segregation to be invalid.

In the fall of 1953 briefs and arguments were presented on these points. On the historical issues the results were entirely inconclusive. Few at the time of the adopting of the Fourteenth Amendment had given any thought to racial segregation in the public schools; in 1868 there were not many public schools, and what few Negroes had ever been admitted to those that did exist were usually accepted in separate schools. There were, however, various suggestions presented as to the form of the Court's possible decree.

In May, 1954, the Court handed down its decision in these five cases and overruled, with respect to public schools, the "separate but equal" doctrine of *Plessy* v. *Ferguson. (Brown* v. *Board of Education,* 347 U.S. 483.) In an opinion in which the Court regarded the sociological and psychological effects of segregation as decisive, the

Court held that the simple fact of segregation in public schools denies the equal protection of the laws. Three aspects of this important decision may be noted: (1) The Court was unanimous; (2) the Court wrote but one opinion, presented by the Chief Justice, thus indicating unanimous agreement on the reasons as well as the results; (3) the Court set for reargument in the 1954 term the whole problem of the methods available to the Court for implementing its decree.

In May, 1955, the Supreme Court handed down its decree to implement its antisegregation decision of 1954. (*Brown* v. *Board of Education,* 349 U.S. 294.) The decree took into account two facts: first, that desegregation will be more difficult in some communities than in others and, second, that the process will take time. The Court ordered that "a prompt and reasonable start toward full compliance with our May 17, 1954, ruling" be made. It left to the federal district courts, however, the duty of supervising the difficult enterprise. These courts may allow extensions of time for carrying out the decree should there be reasonable grounds for doing so. During the entire period of transition, the courts retain full jurisdiction. The Supreme Court, however, is aware of the social upheaval which is bound to attend desegregation in most southern communities, and, under established equitable principles of law, it has permitted reasonably gradual adjustment to its ban on segregation. The rule of gradual adjustment, however, does not apply to state-supported colleges and universities. In March, 1956, the Court ordered the University of Florida to admit a Negro student to its law school "without delay." (*Hawkins* v. *University of Florida,* 350 U.S. 000, 1956.)

4. Implementing the School Segregation Cases

The entire process of desegregation, as it moves forward, is worthy of thorough and continued study. Some of the problems and developments which have already emerged may be noted:

In many communities state and local educational authorities have, without argument or protest, accepted the Court's decision and are affecting the integration of Negro and white children in the same schools. In some cases this has already been done, in others it will be done with a minimum of delay. Most of these communities are in the border states, where the proportion of Negro children is not so great as in the deep South, and where there is more money available to pay for the necessary costs of the transition.

There are many communities in which there will be no defiance of the desegregation decree, but in which the costs of making the change will be extremely heavy, and extensions of time may be reasonably asked for.

In parts of the deep South—Alabama, Georgia, South Carolina, Mississippi—there is open and vociferous defiance. Governors and United States Senators and Representatives from these states bluntly declare that the mixing of Negroes and whites in the schools of their states will never be allowed. Leaders in these states are using their ingenuity to devise ways and means to bypass or frustrate the antisegregation decree. Both Alabama and Virginia have reasserted the doctrine of "interposition," which has no validity but is a hangover from the early days when some states claimed the right to defy the exercise of national authority thought by the states to be unconstitutional.

Mississippi and Alabama have authorized their legislatures to discontinue public schools entirely, and Virginia is in the process of doing so. The plan is to use state money to provide scholarships for pupils who attend segregated schools. Georgia will allow the grant of state and local funds to citizens of the state "for educational purposes" in discharge of all obligation of the state to provide public education. Another device is to arrange school district lines so that segregation will in effect, though not by legal compulsion, be retained on a "voluntary" basis. Senator Thurmond of South Carolina has introduced a bill which would deprive the Supreme Court and the federal courts of appeal of appellate jurisdiction to review the action of any state in the operation of its schools for any other reason than "substantial inequality of physical facilities and other tangible factors." This would allow the states to disregard the segregation decree with impunity.

While the Supreme Court's recent decisions have related to segregation in the public schools, it is clear that in overruling *Plessy* v. *Ferguson,* which after all was a railroad segregation case, it established a judicial doctrine which will carry over into the other fields in which segregation has so long existed. The Court, without writing opinions, has already in effect extended the rule to a segregated municipal housing project, a golf course, an amphitheater in a public park, and public beaches and bathhouses.

B. DISCRIMINATION AGAINST JEWS

At present some anti-Semitism is organized, and a good deal more is not.

There is very much less organized anti-Semitism today than there was back in the thirties. It is still carried on by a few organizations which do not change much in number, size, or the character of their activities. Some of the professionals stay in business for financial reasons: Gerald L. K. Smith is reported to raise close to $200,000 a year. Other groups are manned by fanatical people who believe in the causes they support. There is little evidence of any "network" of operations in this field, but there is some informal co-operation amongst the various groups.

Unorganized anti-Semitism crops up from time to time as situations seem to stimulate it. The attack on the confirmation of Anna Rosenberg as an Assistant Secretary of Defense was apparently motivated by anti-Semitism, although other factors were present. It has been charged that the McCarran-Walter Immigration Act discriminates against Jews, but it is not easy to prove that whatever discrimination has resulted was intentional rather than incidental. The Jew seems to have suffered little, if any, discrimination at the hands of the government.

Nongovernmental discrimination against Jews takes various forms:

1. *Physical Violence and Vandalism*

A few minor examples of this have occurred since the war and in several areas have been repeated. The problem is quite as much one of juvenile delinquency as of racism.

2. *Transportation*

There is no anti-Semitic problem here.

3. *Public Accommodations, Recreation, Amusements*

There is still a good deal of discrimination in this area, especially by resort hotels. The Anti-Defamation League reported in 1952 that there were 675 hotels which fairly openly discriminated against Jews. Many states have passed laws which forbid this kind of discrimination, but these are not easy to enforce where community opinion is not offended by the discrimination.

4. *Education*

Discrimination against Jews in the matter of admission to colleges and universities is still widespread. The measure, and even the fact, of such discrimination is difficult to document since all of the institutions involved operate on some kind of quota basis and do not attempt the total exclusion of Jewish students. In 1948 New York passed the Quinn-Olliffe Fair Educational Practices Law designed to end racial and religious discrimination. Conclusive figures on the results of this law are not available, but it seems to be accomplishing some of its purposes. Medical schools present a difficult problem here because of the very limited total enrollment, but the Jewish enrollment in the medical schools has doubled in the six years since the law went into effect.

5. *Employment*

Anti-Jewish discrimination in employment is very different from anti-Negro discrimination. As a rule Jews are not barred from "blue collar" jobs; Jewish college graduates do experience some discrimination when they seek professional and executive positions in business and industry. Reliable data for measuring the extent of such discrimination are scanty. State FEPC laws have undoubtedly helped, it is hard to say just how much.

6. *Housing*

Discrimination against Jews in housing still remains, though mainly in the matter of buying a home rather than in renting an apartment. There are a very large number of areas in which sales of residences to Jews are forestalled by covenants written into deeds of sale. These tend to be morally binding even though the courts have held that they cannot be enforced in court.

C. DISCRIMINATION AGAINST OTHER RACIAL MINORITIES

Every American is aware that we face problems of racial discrimination affecting Negroes and Jews. He is less conscious of the existence in this country of other minorities and the problems relating to them. These groups are smaller, they are regionally contained, and whatever injustices they may suffer do not make the headlines of the national press.

The problems posed by the many forms of discrimination directed against these racial groups are numerous and complex. They can be dealt with adequately only by the making of adequate studies and analyses in the areas in which the problems exist. It is beyond the scope of this conspectus to do more than mention the more important of these racial groups.

Many years ago the Supreme Court referred to our tribal Indians as "domestic, dependent nations." They have long since ceased to be nations, but the status of "dependency" with all that it implies has never been wholly removed. American citizenship was belatedly conferred upon all American Indians in 1924. Problems relating to our policies in dealing with our Indian population deserve exhaustive study and analysis in an effort to determine to what extent the Indian is denied the rights and privileges enjoyed by other citizens.

In our southwestern states there are a million and a half American citizens of Mexican extraction. They comprise a racial group which has been subjected to various forms of racial discrimination. In addition there is a substantial body of floating Mexican laborers, who enter the country illegally and are known as "wetbacks."

Discrimination against these Asian races dates back many years. It was represented in our Exclusion Acts and our refusal to permit Chinese and Japanese to become naturalized. The west coast states barred aliens ineligible to citizenship from land ownership for many years. (*Supra,* 208.) Recently some of this discrimination has been removed. The ineligibility to American citizenship no longer exists, and the alien land laws have been declared unconstitutional.

SELECTED READINGS

The literature on the American Negro is very extensive. The classic analysis of the Negro problem in this country is Gunner Myrdal, *An American Dilemma,* 2 volumes (New York: Harper, 1944), a monumental study by a distinguished Scandinavian sociologist in collaboration with leading American experts in the field. An admirable historical study is John Hope Franklin, *From Slavery to Freedom: A History of American Negroes* (New York: Knopf, 1947). Progress toward better race relations is portrayed in a symposium edited by Charles S. Johnson, *Into the Main Stream: A Survey of Best Practices in Race Relations in the South* (Chapel Hill: University of North Carolina, 1947). A distinguished southern editor's discussion of the race problem is Hodding Carter, *Southern Legacy* (Baton Rouge: Louisiana State University Press, 1950). For surveys and analyses of legislation in the race relations field see Charles S. Johnson, *Patterns of Negro Segregation* (New York: Harper, 1943); *Civil Rights in the United States, 1953: A Balance Sheet of Group Relations* (New York: American Jewish Congress and NAACP, 1954).

Harry S. Ashmore, *The Negro and the Schools* (Chapel Hill:

University of North Carolina Press, 1954), analyzes the southern school situation and prints the Supreme Court's opinions in the school segregation cases. Herbert Hill and Jack Greenberg, *Citizen's Guide to De-Segregation* (Boston: Beacon Press, 1955), is the work of two men associated with the NAACP. Current happenings in the field of school integration and racial segregation generally may be followed in two objective reporting services recently established. *Southern School News* (Nashville 5, Tenn.) reports all happenings in the school segregation field. *Race Relations Law Reporter* (Vanderbilt University, School of Law, Nashville 5, Tenn.) covers all legal developments in the field including court decisions, state and federal. The annual subscription to each is $2.00.

There are useful books on special facets of the problem of Negro discrimination. Malcolm Ross, *All Manner of Men* (New York: Reynal and Hitchcock, 1948), is an absorbing story of the wartime Fair Employment Practices Commission and its work by the last chairman of that body. A more recent and general treatment of F.E.P.C. is Louis Ruchames, *Race, Jobs and Politics: The Story of the F.E.P.C.* (New York: Columbia University Press, 1953). Lee Nichols, *Breakthrough on the Color Front* (New York: Random House, 1954), discusses the progress made in eliminating racial segregation in the armed forces. Charles Abrams, *Forbidden Neighbors: A Study of Prejudice in Housing* (New York: Harper, 1955), deals with a current race problem of great importance. Wilson Record, *The Negro and the Communist Party* (Chapel Hill: University of North Carolina Press, 1951), is a reliable account of the unsuccessful efforts of the Communists to draw the American Negro into the Party.

Of the numerous books on anti-Semitism may be mentioned Arnold Forster, *A Measure of Freedom* (New York: Doubleday, 1950); and Arnold Forster and Benjamin Epstein, *Cross-Currents* (New York: Doubleday, 1956).

Table of Cases

A.F. of L. *v.* Mann et al., 188 S.W. 2d 276, 1945. 50
A.F. of L. *v.* McAdory, 246 Ala. 1, 1944. 50
A.F. of L. *v.* Reilly, 113 Colo. 90, 1944 50
American Civil Liberties Union *v.* City of Chicago, 3 Ill. 2d 329, 1954. 14
American Communications Association *v.* Douds, 339 U.S. 382, 1950. 50

Bailey *v.* Richardson, 182 Fed. 2d 46, 1950 37
Ballard, United States *v.*
Ballard *v.* United States, 329 U.S. 187, 1946 150
Baltzer et al., United States *v.*
Barrows *v.* Jackson, 346 U.S. 249, 1953 214
Bauer *v.* Acheson, 106 Fed. Supp. 445, 1952 115
Beauharnais *v.* Illinois, 343 U.S. 250, 1952 . . . . 24, 25
Bland, United States *v.*
Blau *v.* United States, 340 U.S. 159, 1950. 143
Bolling *v.* Sharpe, 347 U.S. 497, 1954. 216
Bowe *v.* Secretary of Commonwealth, 320 Mass. Repts. 230, 1946. . 50
Bridges *v.* California, 314 U.S. 252, 1941 . . . . 8, 10
Brown *v.* Board of Education, 347 U.S. 483, 1954 222
Brown *v.* Board of Education, 349 U.S. 294, 1955 223
Brunner *v.* United States, 343 U.S. 918, 1952. 143
Bruno *v.* United States, 308 U.S. 287, 1939 142
Burstyn *v.* Wilson, 343 U.S. 495, 1952. . . . . 13, 17

Calder *v.* Bull, 3 Dallas, 386, 1798. 160
Carroll *v.* Dumont Laboratories, 340 U.S. 929, 1951. 17
CIO, United States *v.*
Cleveland *v.* United States, 329 U.S. 14, 1946 94
Cochran *v.* Louisiana State Board of Education, 281 U.S. 370, 1930 . 100

TABLE OF CASES

Cohnstaedt v. Immigration and Naturalization Service, 339 U.S. 901, 1949 95
Commercial Pictures Corp. v. Regents of University of State of New York, Superior Films, Inc. v. Department of Education of Ohio, 346 U.S. 587, 1954 14
Communist Party of United States v. Subversive Activities Control Board, 351 U.S. 000, 1956 . . . . 6, 176
Construction and General Laborers Union No. 264, United States v.
Coplon v. United States, 191 Fed. 2d 749, 1951 155
Coplon, United States v.
Corrigan v. Buckley, 271 U.S. 323, 1926 214
Craig v. Harney, 331 U.S. 367, 1947 . . . . 8, 10
Crandall v. Nevada, 6 Wall. 35, 1868 112
Crews v. United States, 160 Fed. 2d 746, 1947 126
Cummings v. Missouri, 4 Wall. 277, 1867 162
Cunningham, United States v.

Danskin v. San Diego Unified School District, 28 Cal. 2d 536, 1946 . 62
DeJonge v. Oregon, 299 U.S. 353, 1937 60
Delaney v. United States, 199 Fed. 2d 107, 1952. 10
Dennis v. United States, 341 U.S. 494, 1951 . . . . . . 58–59, 147
Dickinson v. United States, 346 U.S. 389, 1953 98
District of Columbia v. Thompson Co., 346 U.S. 100, 1953 . . . 216
Donaldson v. Read Magazine, 333 U.S. 178, 1948 34
Doremus v. Board of Education, 5 N.J. 435, 1950. 103
  appeal dismissed, 342 U.S. 429, 1952 103
Dorsey v. Stuyvesant Town Corp., 229 N.Y. 512, 1949 220
  certiorari denied, 339 U.S. 981, 1950 220
Douds, American Communications Association v.
Dulles v. Nathan, 225 Fed. 2d 29, 1955 116
Dumont Laboratories v. Carroll, 184 Fed. 2d 153, 1950 17

Edwards v. California, 314 U.S. 160, 1941 112
Ellis v. Dixon, 349 U.S. 458, 1955 62
Esquire, Inc., Hannegan v.
Estep v. United States, 327 U.S. 114, 1946 97
Everson v. Board of Education, 330 U.S. 1, 1947 100

Fay v. New York, 332 U.S. 261, 1947 150
Feiner v. New York, 340 U.S. 315, 1951 58
Frazier v. United States, 335 U.S. 497, 1948 151
Friedman v. New York, 341 U.S. 907, 1951 106–107

Gaines, Missouri ex rel., v. Canada
Garland, Ex parte, 4 Wall. 333, 1867 162

TABLE OF CASES

Girouard v. United States, 328 U.S. 61, 1946 95
Gitlow v. New York, 268 U.S. 652, 1925 1

Hague v. CIO, 307 U.S. 496, 1939 . . . . 60, 63
Hall v. DeCuir, 95 U.S. 485, 1878 217
Hannegan v. Esquire, Inc., 327 U.S. 146, 1946 33
Harris v. United States, 331 U.S. 145, 1947 137
Hartzel v. United States, 322 U.S. 680, 1944 56
Hawaii v. Mankichi, 190 U.S. 197, 1903 57
Hawker v. New York, 170 U.S. 189, 1898 160
Hawkins v. University of Florida, 350 U.S. 000, 1956 223
Henderson v. United States, 339 U.S. 816, 1950 218
Herndon v. Lowry, 301 U.S. 242, 1937 . . . . 4, 56
Holcomb, State ex rel., v. Armstrong
Howarth, People v.
Hurd v. Hodge, 334 U.S. 24, 1948 214

Ingalls, United States v.
International Association of Machinists v. N.L.R.B., 311 U.S. 72, 1940   53

Jelke, People v.

Lanza, United States v.
Lattimore, United States v.
Lawson v. Housing Authority, 70 N.W. 2d 605 173
  certiorari denied, 76 U.S. 135, 1955 173
Louisiana ex rel. Francis v. Resweber, 329 U.S. 459, 1947 157
Lovett, United States v.

Macintosh v. United States, 283 U.S. 605, 1931 95
Maryland v. Baltimore Radio Show, 193 Md. 300, 1949 9–10
  certiorari denied, 338 U.S. 912, 1950 10
Masses Publishing Co. v. Patten, 245 Fed. 102, 1917 32
McAuliffe v. New Bedford, 155 Mass. 216, 1892 28
McCollum v. Board of Education, 333 U.S. 203, 1948 102–103
McGill v. Georgia, 209 Ga. 500, 1953 9
Milwaukee Social Democratic Publishing Co. v. Burleson, 255 U.S. 407,
  1921 32
Missouri ex rel. Gaines v. Canada, 305 U.S. 337, 1938 218
Moore v. Dempsey, 261 U.S. 86, 1923 156
Moore v. Illinois, 14 Howard 13, 1852 158
Morford v. United States, 339 U.S. 258, 1950 151
Morgan v. Commonwealth of Virginia, 328 U.S. 373, 1946 . . . 217
Myers v. United States, 272 U.S. 52, 1926 180

Namba et al., v. McCourt, 185 Ore. 579, 1949 209
Nardone v. United States, 302 U.S. 379, 1937 138
Nathan v. Dulles, 129 Fed. Supp. 951, 1955 116
National Association of Manufacturers v. McGrath, 103 Fed. Supp.
    510, 1952 65
Near v. Minnesota, 283 U.S. 697, 1931 16–17
N.L.R.B. v. Virginia Electric & Power Co., 314 U.S. 469, 1941 . . 53
New American Library of World Literature, Inc. v. Allen, 114 Fed.
    Supp. 823, 1953 16
New Hampshire, by Wyman, Attorney General v. Sweezy, pending in
    the state supreme court 74
Norris v. Alabama, 294 U.S. 587, 1935 151
Nugent, United States v.

Olmstead v. United States, 277 U.S. 438, 1928 137
One Book Entitled Ulysses, United States v.
On Lee v. United States, 343 U.S. 747, 1952 138

Painters Local Union No. 481, United States v.
Palko v. Connecticut, 302 U.S. 319, 1937 57
Parker v. Lester, 227 Fed. 2d 708, 1955 194
Pennekamp v. Florida, 328 U.S. 331, 1946 . . . . 8, 10
Pennsylvania v. Nelson, 377 Pa. 58, 1954 175
Pennsylvania v. Nelson, 350 U.S. 000, 1956 175
People v. Howarth, 415 Ill. 501, 1953 64
People v. Jelke, 308 N.Y. 56, 1954 11
People ex rel. Wallace v. Labrenz, 411 Ill. 618, 1952 93
    certiorari denied, 344 U.S. 824, 1952 93
Pierce v. Society of Sisters, 268 U.S. 510, 1925 102
Pierce v. United States, 146 Fed. 2d 84, 1946, also 157 Fed. 2d 848, 1946 119
    certiorari denied, 329 U.S. 814, 1947 119
Plessy v. Ferguson, 163 U.S. 537, 1896 . . . . . . 217–225 passim
Pollak v. Public Utilities Commission of the District of Columbia, 191
    Fed. 2d 450, 1951 44
    reversed, 343 U.S. 451, 1952 44
Pollock v. Williams, 322 U.S. 4, 1944 118
Porterfield v. Webb, 263 U.S. 225, 1923 209
Provoo, United States v.

Rabinowitz, United States v.
Resweber, Louisiana ex rel. Francis v.
Reynolds v. United States, 98 U.S. 145, 1878 93
Riggins, Ex parte, 134 Fed. 404, 1904 123
R.K.O. Pictures v. Department of Education, 162 Ohio 263, 1954 . 16, 17
Rogers v. United States, 340 U.S. 367, 1951 142

TABLE OF CASES

Ross, *In re*, 140 U.S. 453, 1891 134
Rudder *v.* United States, 226 Fed. 2d 51, 1955 173
Rumely, United States *v.*

Schachtman *v.* Dulles, 225 Fed. 2d 938, 1955 . . . . . 116, 174
Schenck *v.* United States, 249 U.S. 47, 1919 . . . . . 55, 56
Schwimmer *v.* United States, 279 U.S. 644, 1929 95
Sei Fujii *v.* State, 242 Pac. 2d 617, 1952 209
Shelley *v.* Kraemer, 334 U.S. 1, 1948 214
Shepherd *v.* Florida, 341 U.S. 50, 1951 10
Sicurella *v.* United States, 348 U.S. 385, 1955 98
Simmons *v.* United States, 348 U.S. 397, 1955 98
Sipuel *v.* University of Oklahoma, 332 U.S. 631, 1948 . . . 218
Slochower *v.* Board of Education, 351 U.S. 000 144
Smith *v.* Allwright, 321 U.S. 649, 1944 212
State *ex rel.* Holcomb *v.* Armstrong, 39 Wash. 2d 860, 1952 . . 93
Stromberg *v.* California, 283 U.S. 359, 1931 4
Summerfield *v.* Sunshine Book Company, 221 Fed. 2d 42, 1954 . 34
  certiorari denied, 349 U.S. 921, 1955 34
Summers, *in re*, 325 U.S. 561, 1945 96
Sweatt *v.* Painter, 339 U.S. 629, 1950 219

Takahashi *v.* Fish and Game Commission, 334 U.S. 410, 1948 . 209
Taylor *v.* Georgia, 315 U.S. 25, 1942 118
Terminiello *v.* City of Chicago, 337 U.S. 1, 1949 58
Terrace *v.* Thompson, 263 U.S. 197, 1923 209
Thiel *v.* Southern Pacific Company, 328 U.S. 217, 1946 . . . 150
Thomas *v.* Collins, 323 U.S. 516, 1945 . . . . 57, 60
Thornhill *v.* Alabama, 310 U.S. 88, 1940 . . . . . . 52, 56
Tot *v.* United States, 319 U.S. 463, 1943 186
Toth, United States *ex rel., v.* Quarles
Truax *v.* Raich, 239 U.S. 33, 1915 208
Trupiano *v.* United States, 334 U.S. 699, 1948 137
Tucker *v.* Texas, 326 U.S. 517, 1946 36
Tudor *v.* Board of Education, 14 N.J. 31, 1953 104
Tumey *v.* Ohio, 273 U.S. 510, 1927 . . . . 156, 199
Twining *v.* New Jersey, 211 U.S. 78, 1908 142

Ullman *v.* United States, 350 U.S. 000, 1956 145
Ulysses, One Book Entitled, United States *v.*
United Public Workers *v.* Mitchell, 330 U.S. 75, 1947 . . . 28
United States *v.* Ballard, 322 U.S. 78, 1944 . . . . . . 33, 93
United States *v.* Baltzer et al., 248 U.S. 593, 1918 64
United States *v.* Bland, 283 U.S. 636, 1931 95

TABLE OF CASES

United States v. CIO, 77 Fed. Supp. 355, 1948 49
   dismissal affirmed, 335 U.S. 106, 1948 49
United States v. Construction and General Laborers Union No. 264,
   101 Fed. Supp. 869, 1951 49
United States v. Coplon, 185 Fed. 2d 629, 1950. 146
United States v. Cunningham, 40 Fed. Supp. 399, 1941 119
United States v. Ingalls, 73 Fed. Supp. 76, 1947 117
United States v. Lanza, 260 U.S. 377, 1922 159
United States v. Lattimore, 112 Fed. Supp. 507, 1953; *also* 127 Fed.
   Supp. 405, 1955 149
United States v. Lovett, 328 U.S. 303, 1946 163
United States v. Nugent, 346 U.S. 1, 1953 98
United States v. One Book Entitled Ulysses, 72 Fed. 2d 705, 1934 . 38
United States v. Painters Local Union No. 481, 172 Fed. 2d 854, 1949 49
United States v. Provoo, 215 Fed. 2d 531, 1955 153
   affirmed, 350 U.S. 857, 1955 153
United States v. Rabinowitz, 339 U.S. 56, 1950. 137
United States v. Rumely, 345 U.S. 41, 1953 65
United States *ex rel.* Toth v. Quarles, 350 U.S. 11, 1955 133

Vidal v. Girard's Executors, 2 Howard 127, 1844 106
Virginia v. Rives, 100 U.S. 313, 1880 151

Walker v. Popenoe, 149 Fed. 2d 511, 1945 35
Wallace, People *ex rel.*, v. Labrenz
Watkins v. United States, 000 Fed. 2d 000, 1956 181
Weeks v. United States, 232 U.S. 383, 1914 136
Western Union Tel. Co. v. Kansas, 216 U.S. 1, 1910 37
Weston v. Commonwealth, 195 Va. 175, 1953 9
Wieman v. Updegraff, 344 U.S. 183, 1952 . . . . . . 96, 179
Williams v. United States, 341 U.S. 97, 1951 126
Winters v. New York, 333 U.S. 507, 1948 13
Wolf v. Colorado, 338 U.S. 25, 1949 136
Wong Yang Sung v. McGrath, 339 U.S. 33, 1950 35

Zorach v. Clauson, 343 U.S. 306, 1952 103

Index

AAUP, *see* American Association of University Professors

Academic freedom: chapter on, 70–90; blacklisting of teachers, 83; censorship of academic activities, 73–75, 85–86; classified research, 86–87; in colleges and universities, 71–72; congressional investigation of, 83–84; dangers from financial supporters, 72, 87–89; definitions of, 70; disloyalty of teachers, 80–82; dismissal of teachers, 77, 81–84, 144; outside pressure groups, 89–90; political activities of teachers, 75–76; in public schools, 73; tenure of teachers, 76–77; textbooks, teaching materials, curriculum, 75, 85–86

ACLU, *see* American Civil Liberties Union

Adams, John, 153

Administrative Procedure Act, 1946, 34–35

Advocacy, crimes of, 3–5, 50–52, 175; *see also* Smith Act

AFL, 50

Alabama: to discontinue public schools, 225; interposition, 224; statute on protection of news sources, 225

Alien land laws, unconstitutional, 208–209, 229

Alien Registration Act, 1940, 176

Aliens: chapter on, 208–210; admission of, 161; civil liberties of, 208; denied visas, 209; enemy, 128; exclusion of, 168; fingerprinting, 168, 176; and lynching, 121; registration of, 168, 176; treaty rights of, 121, 208

American Association of University Professors (AAUP), on academic freedom, 90

American bar, as defense counsel, 154

American Bar Association, 198

American citizenship: of conscientious objectors, 95; given Indians, 228

American Civil Liberties Union (ACLU): on blacklisting by radio networks, 43; on group libel legislation, 25; on student freedom, 77

American Council of Education, 78

American Federation of Labor (AFL), 50

American Indians, 228

American Jewish Congress, on group libel legislation, 25

American Legion, 67, 89, 131, 202

Anarchists, 154, 168

Anti-Communist laws, 200

Antidiscrimination provisions: in government contracts, 212–213; laws of states, 215

Antihate legislation, 23

Anti-Semitism, 225

Antisyndicalism, 175

Arizona, and polygamy, 94

INDEX

Armed forces: censorship in, 29–30; Negroes in, 211, 220–221
Arrest, section on, 146–147
Artists, denied visas, 210
Asians: barred from land ownership, 208; discrimination against, 229
Assembly, freedom of, 63
Atomic Energy Act, 1946, 131, 167
Atomic Energy Commission, and conscientious objectors, 96
Attorney General: and emergency detention, 129; memorandum on NATO Status of Forces Agreement, 133; power to exclude aliens, 168; on wiretapping, 139–140
Attorney General's Committee on Administrative Procedure, 34
Attorney General's list of subversive organizations, 80, 116, 154, 170–171, 173–174, 183, 188, 200

Bail, 147
Banishment, as penalty for crime, 113
Bar associations, in defense of Communists, 154
Bible reading, in public schools, 103–104
Bill of Rights: does not apply outside the country, 133–134; of Great Britain (1689) and legislative immunity, 21; provisions assimilated into Fourteenth Amendment, 57
Bills of attainder, 162–163
Black, Hugo L., Justice, 58; dissent in Dennis case, 59; on racial discrimination, 220
Blacklisting: by private organizations, 203; in radio and television, 43, 203; of teachers, 83
Blanshard, Paul, 106
Blue Book, issued by FCC, 43
Blue ribbon jury, 150
Board of Passport Appeals, 115
Boycotts, in aid of censorship, 67
Brandeis, Louis D., Justice: on right to privacy, 25–26; on separation of powers, 180
Broadcasting: of courtroom or legislative committee proceedings, 44; of defamatory material, 43–44; self-censorship of industry, 19, 40, 44–45, 66; as treason, 3, 164; *see also* Radio
Bryan, William Jennings, 75–76
Butler, J. M., Senator, proposes security bill, 172

Cairns, Huntington, 18, 38
California: bars UNESCO publications, 86; espionage in schools and colleges, 83; law on interstate movement of indigent, 112; loyalty oath in, 174; Institute of Technology, 115; Tenney Committee, 188, 190; use of school buildings by subversive groups, 61
Capital punishment, 159
"Captive audience," 44
Carr, Robert K., President's Committee on Civil Rights, 213
Catholic church: Legion of Decency, 66; *see also* Parochial schools
Censor, competence of, 18
Censorship: and academic freedom, 73–74; in the armed services, 29–30; in broadcasting industry, 17, 19, 39–40, 66; of comic books, 12, 14; by customs authorities, 18, 38; of films, shows, theaters, 12–18, 59; of literature, 12–18, 38, 59, 85–86; of official speech, 29–30; in overseas libraries, 45–48; postal, 5, 7, 30–37; private, 15, 66–68; by states, 12–14; of student publications, 78; of textbooks, 85–86; vagueness in laws on, 13, 148; *see also* Obscenity
Central Intelligence Agency, 167
Champaign (Ill.), released-time program, 102
Chicago (Ill.), ordinance against racial discrimination, 216
Chief of Religious Information, office created, 107
Child benefit theory, 100–102
Chinese, discrimination against, 208, 229
Christian Scientists, and religious liberty, 93, 106
Church and state, separation of, section on, 99–107

INDEX

Cicero (Ill.), race riot in, 221
CIO, *see* Congress of Industrial Organizations
Civil liberties, *see specific topics listed in this Index and Table of Contents*
Civil rights, federal protection of, 124–128
Civil Rights Act, 16, 63, 124, 126, 136
Civil Rights Program, 1946, 213
Civil Rights Section (Justice Dept.): section on, 124–128; peonage case, 118; police brutality, 146
Clark, Grenville, quoted, 89
Clark, Mark, National Council for American-Soviet Friendship, 188
Classics, importation of, 38
Classification Act, 33
Classification of documents, 6, 167
Classified research, in colleges and universities, 86–87
Clear and present danger doctrine, 55–59
Coast Guard, security provisions in, 194
Colleges and universities: discrimination against Jews in, 227; segregation in, 218–219; *see also* Academic freedom
Columbia University, and outside speakers, 78
Comic books, 12, 14
Commerce, Dept. of, Office of Strategic Information and official secrecy, 7
Common law, religion in, 106
Communism: section on program to combat, 167–177; and academic freedom, 80–81; private activities against, 177, 201–205; and self-incrimination, 142–144
Communist: action organizations denied passports, 114; books in overseas libraries, 45–48; front organizations, 176; lawyers, 154; leaders, eleven (Dennis *et al.*), 147, 159; registration of organizations, 175
Communist Control Act, 1954, 42, 51, 172
Communist Party: a criminal conspiracy, 59; members barred from naturalization, 168; membership and passports, 115; membership and self-incrimination, 142; membership and Taft-Hartley Act, 50–52; membership and teachers, 81; state disabilities, 171
Communists: barred from country, 168; barred from naturalization, 169; counsel for, 154, 191; denied passports, 115; excessive bail for, 147; excessively heavy penalties for, 158; exposure of, 177–205 *passim;* infiltration of labor unions by, 50–52, 172; infiltration of organizations by, 176; infiltration of schools and colleges by, 89; literature by, 5; radio broadcasts by, 5, 42; use of public buildings by, 61; *see also* Loyalty oaths
Confrontation of witnesses, 155–156, 192–194
Congress: and Civil Rights Program, 213; power to make rules for its committees, 194, 198; power over segregation in District of Columbia and interstate transportation, 212, 216–218
Congressional immunity, 21
Congressional investigating committees, *see* Legislative investigating committees
Congress of Industrial Organizations (CIO): *News,* 49; Political Action Committee, 50; political spending, 48–50
Conscientious objectors: section on, 94–99; in colleges, 79; and double jeopardy, 98, 159
"Constructive" treason, 163
Contempt of court: section on, 8–11; and clear and present danger, 56; and right of petition, 64
Coplon, Judith: arrested without warrant, 146; right to counsel, 155; wiretap evidence, 139–140
Corporations: aid to education, 88; political spending, 48
Counsel: for Communists, 154, 191; as essential to fair trial, 110; for passport applicants, 115; right to, 153–155

Counterattack, 203, 204
Counterespionage, 167
Court martial, 132; of conscientious objectors, 99
Court of Military Appeals, 132
Courts, press criticism of, 8–11
Covenants, restrictive, 214–215
Coy, Wayne, 40
Criminal Code, 39, 133
Criminal conspiracy, and clear and present danger, 58–59
Criminal justice, 135–164
Cross-examination of witnesses, 155
Cruel and unusual punishments, 157–158
Customs authorities, censorship by, 38

DAR, 67, 202
Daughters of the American Revolution, 67, 202
Davis, John W., 154
Davis, Kenneth, quoted, 41
Defamation, in broadcasting programs, 43–44; *see also* Libel
Defense, Dept. of: contracts with universities, 87; loyalty oaths for ROTC, 173; and Negro segregation, 220; secrecy rules, 7
Delaware, law on political spending, 50
Denaturalization, 161, 169
Denominational schools, and academic freedom, 71
Deportation: a civil proceeding, 161; Immigation and Nationality Act, 1952, 169; of subversive aliens, 176
Desegregation, problems of, 224–225
Detention: section on emergency detention, 128, 129; Review Board, 129
Dickstein, Samuel, bill introduced by, 23
Dies, Martin, 180, 187
Dies Committee, 180, 182, 190
Discharge from the armed forces, "undesirable" and "general," 185
Disclosure and registration: section on, 5; of subversives, 175
Discrimination: against aliens, 208–210; against conscientious objectors, 95; *see also* Racial discrimination

Disfranchisement of Negroes, 212
Disloyalty: and academic freedom, 80–83; and bills of attainder, 162–163; of criticism and dissent, 190; programs directed against, 169–172; standards for determining, 181–185
District of Columbia: loyalty oath in, 174; Negro segregation in, 212, 216
Dodd, William E., Jr., bill of attainder against, 162, 187
Double jeopardy, 158–159
Douglas, William O., Justice: Craig case, 8; dissent in Dennis case, 59; on First Amendment rights, 58; grants stay to Rosenbergs, 191; racial discrimination, 220; resolution to impeach, 191
Draft, evasion of (Espionage Act, 1917), 2, 56
Draftees, security procedures affecting, 185
Due process of law: and cruel punishments, 157–158; and establishment of religion, 99–107; and fair trial, 110, 150, 156; and forced confessions, 145–146; and legislative hearings, 198; and lynching, 123; and notice and hearing, 35, 115; includes parts of Bill of Rights, 57; requires clear definition of crimes, 13, 148–149, 181, 185; and right to counsel, 153; and right to passport, 116; and televising trials, 44; as test of free speech, 59; and unreasonable searches, 136

Eastland, James O., loyalty oath for lawyers, 173
Edgerton, Henry W., Judge, dissent in Bailey case, 37
"Editoralizing" over radio, 41–42
Education, *see* Academic freedom
Eighth Amendment: section on cruel and unusual punishments, 157–158; forbids excessive bail, 147
Eisenhower, Dwight D.: on declaring martial law, 132; on discrimination in the armed forces, 220; on discrimination in government contracts, 214; "don't join the book-burners," 47;

INDEX

and National Council for American-Soviet Friendship, 188; order on classification of documents, 167; security program, 170
Eisenhower Security Order, 1953, 170, 183–185, 192
Emergency detention, 128–129
Employers, free speech of, 53–54
Employment, public, as a privilege, 28
Espionage: laws against, 175; in schools and colleges, 83; in time of emergency, 129; under Truman Loyalty Order, 183
Espionage Act, 1917, 2, 167, 175
Establishment of religion, *see* Separation of church and state
Evidence, section on securing of, 135–146; in hearings on dismissal of teachers, 77; and right of confrontation, 155; by wiretapping inadmissible, 139
Exclusion acts against Asians, 229
Exclusion of aliens deemed subversive, 168
Ex-Communists, as witnesses, 196
Ex post facto laws: section on, 160–162; and wiretap evidence, 140
Exposure of Communists and subversives, 178–180; by legislative committees, 180–181

Fair comment, in the law of libel, 22
Fair Educational Practices Law, 227
Fair Employment Practices Committee, 216; wartime, 212
Fair Employment Practices program, 213
Fair Labor Standards Act, enforcement, 127
Fair trial: and a free press, 9–11; required by due process, 150, 156
Faith-healing, illegal in states, 93
Faribault plan, Catholic schools under, 104
Fascists, and use of public buildings, 61
FBI, *see* Federal Bureau of Investigation
Federal aid to education, 88
Federal Bureau of Investigation (FBI): aids Civil Rights Section, 126; can tap wires, 139; on college campuses, 83; and confidential informers, 193; and counterespionage, 167; records denied to Congress, 197; reports in conscientious objector hearings, 98; review of loyalty cases, 170
Federal Communications Act, 1934, 19, 42–43, 138
Federal Communications Commission: allocation of time, 42; *Blue Book*, 43; and censorship, 19, 39–40, 43; on Communist broadcasting, 42; Mayflower decision on editorializing, 41; on liability for defamation, 43
Federal housing units, subversives barred from, 173, 176
Federal Loyalty Security Program, *see* Loyalty-security programs
Federal Public Housing Authority, and religious literature, 36
Feinberg Act, N.Y., 82
FEPC, 216; wartime, 212
Ferguson, Homer, Senator, 49
Fifth Amendment: books by those who plead, 46; and grand jury indictment, 147; as invoked by teachers, 84; not applicable to states, 142, 148; self-incrimination clause, 140–144
Fines, excessive, 157
Fingerprinting, of aliens, 168, 176
First Amendment rights: and academic freedom, 70, 73; and censorship, 13, 16, 60; and contempt of court, 8; controversial meetings, 62; and internal security, 29; and labor relations, 48; and libel, 25; not absolute, 2; and police power, 26; and postal censorship, 33; "preferred status" of, 56–57; private restrictions on, 66–68, 203; as privilege, section on, 30–48; in radio, 43; and religion, 92–107 *passim;* and secrecy, 6; and sedition, 4; Supreme Court on, 55–60; *see also* Assembly, Petition, Press, Religion, Speech
Florida, University of, ordered to admit Negro, 223
Forced confessions, 145–146

Foreign Agents Registration Act, 1940, 5, 175
Foreign propaganda, censorship of, 37
Fourteenth Amendment, does not apply to individuals, 124; *see also* Due process of law *and* Racial discrimination
Fourth Amendment, unreasonable searches and seizures, 135–138
France, libel in, 23
Frankfurter, Felix: concurred in Dennis case, 59; on fair trial, 9; on First Amendment rights, 58; on procedure, 191; quoted, 135, 191
Freedom, *see* Academic freedom, Assembly, Person, Petition, Press, Religion, Speech
"Friendly witnesses," 196
Fugitive Felon Act, 1934, 118

Garland, A. H., and bill of attainder, 162
Gellhorn, Walter, quoted, 3
Georgia: peonage in, 119; and school segregation, 225
German American Bund, 24
Germany, libel in, 23
Gideon Society, 104
Gold Star Mothers, requires loyalty oath, 202
Grand jury indictment, 147–148
Great Britain: injunctions in libel cases, 20; and legislative immunity, 21; newspaper reporting of criminal proceedings, 9–10; Star Chamber, 152
Group libel, 23–25
Guilt by association: section on, 185–191; and counsel for Communists, 154; and freedom of assembly, 62; and right of petition, 65
Guilt by coincidence, 189
Gwinn Amendment, 173

Habeas corpus: section on, 109–112; in arrests, 146
Hammett, Dashiell, 47
Hand, Learned, Judge, on clear and present danger, 59
Harvard University, academic freedom in, 78, 88
Hatch Act, 1939, 28–29, 127, 170
Hawaii, military government in, 112, 131
Hearings: on dismissal of teachers, 77; under emergency detention, 129; for passport applicants, 115; in postal censorship, 34
Hiss, Alger, 176, 191
Holmes, Oliver Wendell, Justice: clear and present danger, 55, 57; McAuliffe case, 28
Hoover, J. Edgar, 197
Hotels, racial discrimination in, 215, 226
House Committee on Un-American Activities: lists organizations, 200; membership sought in, 199; procedures in, 194, 198
Housing, 173, 176, 219–220
Hughes, Charles E., Justice, free speech cases, 59

Illinois: conscientious objectors, 95; group libel law, 25
Immigration: of dangerous aliens, 168, 176; proceedings are civil, 161
Immigration and Nationality Act, 1952, 95, 168, 176, 209, 226
Immunity Act, 1954, held constitutional, 145
Indiana: group libel law, 24; loyalty oath in, 174; on screening textbooks, 86
Indians, discrimination against, 228
Indictment, by grand jury, 147–148
Injunctions, in libel cases, 20
Interdepartmental Committee on Employee Loyalty, 170
Internal Security Act, 1950, 114, 128, 168, 176, 210
International Information Agency, 45
Interposition, doctrine of in southern states, 224
Interstate commerce: and censorship, 19; freedom to travel in, 112; segregation in, 216–218
Interstate Commerce Act, 1887, and segregation, 217

INDEX

Into the Main Stream, by Charles S. Johnson, cited, 221
Involuntary servitude, 117–119
Ives-Quinn Act, 1945, 215

Jackson, Robert H., Justice: on clear and present danger, 59; on fair trial, 10; on freedom to travel, 112
Japanese, discrimination against, 208, 229
Japanese-American evacuation, 128
Jehovah's Witnesses: as conscientious objectors, 98; and group libel law, 24; and religious liberty, 93, 94
Jenner, William E., on subversion in colleges, 83
Jeopardy, double, 98, 159
Jersey City, ban on public meetings, 60
Jews: and Bible reading, 104; censorship by, 67; discrimination against, 225–228
Johnson, Charles S., *Into the Main Stream,* 221
Judicial Conference of the United States, on habeas corpus, 111
Judicial review: of draft board orders, 97; *in re* passports, 115; of postal censorship, 36
Jury: trial by, section on, 149–153; grand jury, 147–148
Justice, Dept. of, *see* Civil Rights Section *and* Federal Bureau of Investigation

Kansas, repeals censorship law, 17
Kansas State Teachers College, dismisses teachers, 82
Kickback Act, 127
Kidnaping: Lindbergh Act, 126; and wiretaps, 140
King James Bible, 104
Ku Klux Klan, 24, 126

Labor-Management Relations Act, *see* Taft-Hartley Act
Labor unions: Communist infiltration of, 50–51; political spending by, 48; restrict free speech of members, 54–55

Lattimore, Owen, 149
Legion of Decency, 66
Legislative immunity, 21
Legislative investigating committees: section on procedures of, 194–198; confrontation of witnesses, 156; and exposure of subversives, 180; immunity from libel, 21; and presumptions of guilt, 187–190; and schools and colleges, 83
Libel: section on, 19–26; group libel, 23–25; in radio and television, 43–44
Libraries, censorship: of overseas, 45–48; of school, 85–86
Licensing of broadcasting stations, 40
Lindbergh Kidnaping Act, 126
Lippmann, Walter, quoted, 179
Lobbying, and the right of petition, 65
London Daily Mirror, contempt of court, 9
Lorwin, Val, 148
Louisiana: criminal libel case, 22; and free textbooks, 100
Lovett, Robert A., quoted, 201
Lovett, Robert Morss, 162, 187
Lowell, A. Lawrence, on academic freedom, 74
Loyalty boards, *see* Security boards
Loyalty oaths: section on federal and state, 171, 172–174, 176; for conscientious objectors, 96; private, 202; for teachers, 80–81
Loyalty Review Board, 192
Loyalty-security programs, sections on, 169–172, 182–185, 192–194
Lynching: section on, 120–123; and Civil Rights Section, 126–127

MacArthur, Douglas, and National Council for American-Soviet Friendship, 188
Magnuson Act, 1950, 194
Mails, *see* Postal censorship
Mann Act, 94, 119
Marshall, George C., and National Council for American-Soviet Friendship, 188
Martial law, 112, 132
Maryland, Ober law, 171

Massachusetts: and group libel, 24; law on political spending, 50
Mayflower decision, 41
McCarran-Walter Immigration Act, 1952, 95, 168, 176, 209, 226
McCarthy, Joseph R., broadcasts by, 43
McReynolds, James C., Justice, quoted, 88
Mexicans: discrimination against, 228; victims of peonage, 118
Military power and civil liberty: section on, 131–134; and conscientious objectors, 96–99
"Miracle, The," 13, 14
Mississippi, and desegregation, 225
Morgenthau, Henry, Jr., 38
Mormons, and polygamy, 93, 94
Motion pictures, censorship of: by government, 13, 16, 59; by private groups, 66
Murphy, Frank, creates Civil Rights Section, 125
Murray, Philip, on labor's political spending, 49
Mutual Security Agency, 46

NAACP, 67
Nathan, Otto, passport case, 116
Nation, The, barred from school libraries, 106
National Association for the Advancement of Colored People (NAACP), and censorship, 67
National Association of Radio and Television Broadcasters, censorship by, 45
National Council for American-Soviet Friendship, 188
National Gallery of Art, secretary of, and custom censorship, 18, 38
National Labor Relations Board (NLRB), free speech and labor relations, 50
National Lawyers Guild, 154
National security: chapter on, 166–205; immunity of witnesses, 144; and secrecy, 6; and subversive literature, 7; and visas for aliens, 209; and wiretapping, 140

NATO Status of Forces Agreement, 133–134
Naturalization: a civil proceeding, 161; subversives denied, 168
Nazi saboteurs, captured by wiretap, 139
Negroes: censorship by, 67; discrimination against, section on, 211–225; and group libel, 25; held in slavery (1954), 117; on juries, 150; lynching of, 120; peonage, 118
New Jersey, group libel law, 24
Newspaper reporters, protection of news sources, 11
Newspapers, and privileged statements, 21
Newsreels, not censored, 17
New York: blue ribbon jury, 150; loyalty oaths, 174; prayer in schools, 106; on screening textbooks, 86
New York Criminal Anarchy Act, 1902, 4
New York laws: on habitual criminals, 162; on libel in radio and television, 44; on loyalty of teachers (Feinberg Act), 82; on obscenity, 13; on practice of medicine *(Hawker* v. *New York),* 160; on racial and religious discrimination, 215, 227; on released time in schools, 103; on right of privacy, 26; on Sunday observance, 106
New York City: bans *The Nation* in schools, 106; and Christian Scientists, 106; requires teachers to inform, 82; wiretapping scandals, 140
New York Security Risk Act, 1951, 171
NLRB, 50
Non-Communist affidavit, 50–52

Oaths, *see* Loyalty oaths *and* Test oaths
Ober, Frank, 88
Ober law, Maryland, 171
Obscenity: section on, 12–19; in broadcasting, 19, 39–41; censorship by minority groups, 66–67; in District of Columbia, 19; in importations, 18, 38; in interstate commerce, 19; in mails, 18–19; standards and definitions, 12–14; state and local procedures, 14–18; *see also* Postal censorship

INDEX

Office of Strategic Information (Commerce Dept.), 7
Ohio, loyalty oath in, 174
Ohio State University, ban on outside speakers, 74, 85
Oklahoma, loyalty oath, 96
One-man committee hearings, 197
"Operation Alert," 132
Oppenheimer, Robert, barred from speaking, 85
Overseas libraries, censorship in, 45-58
Overthrow of government: state laws against advocacy of, 3-5, 175; Taft-Hartley Act, 50-52; *see also* Smith Act

Parochial schools: merged with public schools, 104-105; state aid to, 100-102; *see also* Separation of church and state
Passport: right to, section on, 113-116; denied to subversives, 176
Pauling, Linus, passport, 115
Peace Information Center, 5
Pennsylvania: and dismissal of teachers, 82; law on political spending, 50; sedition law invalid, 175
Pensions, denied subversives, 176
Peonage: section on, 117-119; and Civil Rights Section, 125
Perjury: Lattimore case, 149; Lorwin case, 148
Pershing, John, National Council for American-Soviet Friendship, 188
Person, freedom of, chapter on, 109-130
Persons accused of crime, rights of, chapter on, 135-165
Petition, freedom of, section on, 63-65
Philadelphia, FEPC ordinance, 216
Picketing, 52, 56, 62-63
Pittsburgh, FEPC ordinance, 216
Police brutality, 126, 145, 156
Police power: assembly, 60-63; freedom of religion, 92; public morals, 12; speeches and canvassing, 26
Political Action Committee, CIO, 50
Political broadcasts, may not be censored, 42
Polygamy, 93, 94

Postal censorship: section on, 30-37; foreign mail, 7; foreign political propaganda, 5
Presidential amnesty for conscientious objectors, 96
President's Committee on Civil Rights: and Civil Rights Section, 128; creation and work of, 213; on group libel legislation, 25; on lynching, 121
President's Committee on Government Contract Compliance, 213-214
Press, freedom of: chapter on, 2-60 *(see Table of Contents)*; and academic freedom, 73-74; in the courts, 55-60; private curbs on, 66-68
Presumptions of guilt (guilt by association), section on, 185-191
Prior censorship, *see* Censorship
Privacy, right of, 25-26
Privilege, doctrine of, 30-48 *passim*
Privileged statements in law of libel, 20-22
Public defenders, proposal for, 153
Public schools: loyalty oaths in, 80; merged with parochial schools, 104-105; religious instruction in, 102-104; segregation in, 219, 221-225; tax-supported, 73; textbooks and curriculum, 75
Public trial, *see* Trial
Punishment, cruel and unusual, section on, 157-158
Punitive exposure, of subversives, 199

Quincy, Josiah, 153
Quinn-Olliffe Fair Educational Practices Law, 227

Racial discrimination: chapter on, 211-229
against Asians, 229; against Indians, 228; against Jews, 225-228; against Mexicans, 228
against Negroes, section on, 211-225
in the armed forces, 211, 220; in the District of Columbia, 212, 216; group libel, 25; in industry (FEPC), 212-213; in interstate transportation, 216; lynchings, 120-121; in

246 INDEX

the North, 212; in public housing units, 219–220; restrictive covenants, 214–215; school segregation cases (1945–1953), 218–219, and (1954), 221–225; state laws against, 215–216; in voting, 127, 212

Radio: section on, 39–45; allocation of time, 42–43; blacklisting by, 43, 203; broadcasts by Communists, 42; censorship of, 17, 19, 39–40, 66; "editorializing," 41–42; liability for libel, 20, 43–44; licensed by FCC, 41–42

Railway Labor Act (Civil Rights Section), 127

Red Channels, 204

Registration: of aliens, 176; of foreign agents, 5, 175

Released-time program, 102–103

Religion, chapter on, 92–107

freedom of, section on, 92–99

and antisocial conduct, 92–94; and conscientious objectors, 94–99; enjoys preferred status, 94

separation of church and state, section on, 99–107

government recognition of, 106–107; instruction in public schools, 102–104; mergers of sectarian and public schools, 104–105; state aid to parochial schools, 100–102

Religious discrimination, New York law against, 215

Restrictive covenants, 214–215

"Right to Privacy," in *Harvard Law Review,* 26

Rosenberg, Anna, 226

Rosenberg case: conviction, 167; Justice Douglas and, 191; picketing in, 63

ROTC, and loyalty oath, 173

Rutledge, Wiley B., Justice, 57

Sabotage, 128, 182

Safety Appliance Act, Civil Rights Section, 127

Sarah Lawrence College, academic freedom in, 89

Schools: censorship of libraries, 85–86; congressional investigations of, 83–84; *see also* Academic freedom, Colleges, Parochial schools, *and* Public schools

Scientists, denied visas, 210

Scopes trial, 75

Searches and seizures, unreasonable, 135–138

Second-class mailing privileges, *see* Postal censorship

Secrecy rules: of government information, 6–7; and internal security, 167; in university research, 86–87

Security boards: section on procedures of, 192–194, *also* 187; confrontation of witnesses, 156; pressures on, 200

Security of the person, chapter on, 109–129 *(see Table of Contents)*

Security Order of 1953, 170, 183–185, 192

Security programs, *see* Loyalty-security programs

Security risks, *see* Loyalty-security programs

Sedition, 3–5, 175; state law on held invalid, 175; *see also* Smith Act

Sedition Act, 1798, 3

Segregation, *see* Racial discrimination

Selective Service Acts, 96–98

Self-incrimination: in investigations of communism and subversion, 142–143; invoked by teachers, 84–85; judicial rules governing, 141–142; reprisals upon pleaders of, 144

"Separate but equal" doctrine, 218–219, 221–222

Separation of church and state, section on, 99–107

Separation of powers, and exposure of subversives, 180–181

Sixth Amendment: confrontation of witnesses, 155–156; counsel, right to, 153–155; jury trial, 149–153

Slander, *see* Libel

Slavery, 117, 125

Smith, Gerald L. K., anti-Semitic activities, 226

Smith Act, 1940, 3, 58, 143, 147, 168, 175

Smith-Connally Act, 1943, 48

Sound trucks, 27, 58

INDEX

South Carolina, Thurmond bill, 225
South Dakota, farmers' petition against draft, 64
Speech, freedom of; governmental restrictions of, 2–55; in the courts, 55–60; private curbs on, 66–68 *(see Table of Contents, ch. I)*
Speedy trial, 152
State, Dept. of: and alien visas, 209–210; Board of Passport Appeals and issuance of passports, 113–116; censorship of overseas libraries, 45–48
Stone, Harlan F., Justice, free speech cases, 59
Story, Joseph, Justice, quoted, 106
Students, freedom for, 77–79
Stuyvesant Town, racial discrimination, 220
Subversion: chapter on, 166–205 *(see Table of Contents);* see also Subversives
Subversive Activities Control Act, 1950, 5, 63
Subversive literature barred: from country, 7–8; from mails, 7–8; from overseas libraries, 45–48
Subversive organizations, *see* Attorney General's list *and* Subversive Activities Control Act
Subversives: barred from public housing units, 173, 176; barred from public office, 161; disabilities, 176; disclosure requirements, 175; exposure of, 179–180, 198–201; private action against, 201–205; punishments, 157–158; and self-incrimination, 142–144; teachers' oaths, 80–82; use of public buildings, 61
Sunday laws, 106–107
"Supreme Being clause," 97

Taft-Hartley Act, 1947: on free speech of employers, 53–54; and labor, 48–52; non-Communist affidavit, 50–52; picketing, 52; political spending, 48–50
Teachers, *see* Academic freedom
Television, *see* Radio
Tennessee, antievolution law, 75

Tenney Committee, California, 188, 190
Test oaths, 172, 174; for teachers, 80; *see also* Loyalty oaths
Texas: loyalty oaths for authors and publishers, 86, 174, and for students, 72; murder trial televised, 44
"Third degree," *see* forced confessions
Thirteenth Amendment, peonage and slavery, 117–119
Thomas, J. Parnell, quoted, 182, 190, 194
Thurmond bill, 225
Touhy, Roger, 110
Treason: section on, 163–164; defined, 3; in Truman Loyalty Order, 183
Treaty rights: of aliens, 208; in early antilynching legislation, 124
Trial: section on, 149–153; press coverage, 9–11
Truman, Harry S.: on contract appliance, 213; appoints ambassador to Vatican, 107; creates first loyalty program, 170; creates President's Committee on Civil Rights, 213; desegregation in armed forces, 220; order to classify documents, World War II, 6; pardons Selective Service Act offenders, 96; vetoes Immigration and Nationality Act of 1952, 209
Truman Loyalty Order, 1947, 170, 182–183, 192
Tucker, John Randolph, quoted, 154

Ulysses, importation upheld, 38
Unconstitutional conditions, doctrine of, 37
UNESCO, publications barred in California, 86
Uniform Code of Military Justice, 132
United Automobile Workers (CIO), and political spending, 49
Unreasonable searches and seizures, 135–138

Vagueness, in criminal statutes, 13, 59, 148–149, 181–182
Vatican, ambassador to, 107
Vigilantism, 201–205
Vinson, Fred M.: on clear and present

danger, Dennis case, 59
Virginia: on interposition, 224; law on segregation on interstate buses, 217
Visas: of aliens, 209; of scientists, 210; of subversives, 176

Wagner Act, 53, 63
Warrants: in arrests, 146; in searches, 147
War Relocation Centers, 128
Washington, D.C., segregation in, 212, 216
Washington, University of: bars speech by Oppenheimer, 85; requires chest X-ray, 93
Washington Post, quoted, 47
Watson, Goodwin B., bill of attainder against, 162, 187
Watts, Rowland, study by, 185

West Virginia, sedition law, 4
Wetbacks, 229
White House, picketing of, 63
Willkie, Wendell, defended Communist William Schneiderman, 154
Wilson, Charles E., 213
Wiretapping, section on, 138–140
Wisconsin, University of, outside speakers, 78
Witnesses: before investigating committees, 195–196; confrontation of, 155–156, 192–194

Yonkers (N.Y.) Board of Education, bars controversial meeting, 62
Youngdahl, Luther W., and Lattimore case, 149
Youngstown, Ohio, censorship by police, 15